The Sorrow of Mary

Written by Collin May

ISBN: 1-4107-6463-X (e-book)
ISBN: 1-4107-6464-8 (Paperback)

This book is printed on acid free paper.

1stBooks – rev. 07/11/03

Preface

Who to thank for their help in writing this? I will start with the Lord Almighty who gives me the strength to stay awake at night so that I may focus on those things that I feel strongly about. God gives strengths in more forms than can be imagined and in those times that I feel too tired to go on, too sleepy to work, or too disheartened to care about my work, He always finds a way to refill my strength and remind me of my goals. With His strength I have found my own. Next, I will thank my best friend Stephan. He showed me that good writing needed more than good content. He reminds me constantly that giving to others is more important than what we give to ourselves, and any act for the benefit of a stranger is an act for the benefit of mankind. Also I wish to thank Galen Farrington. He taught me the power of positive thinking, and has guided me more than he could know. Finally, there is another person to give my thanks, and in such, I dedicate this novel to that person. This person taught me that doing something great means nothing if those whom you care about do not benefit from it. This person taught me that when working on those things that matter, a half way job could never cut it. This person who constantly forces me to do my best, also reminds me how important it is. This book is dedicated to that person that always did whatever it took to help me. This book is dedicated to that person that taught me the skills to be stronger than I ever thought I could be. This book is dedicated to the most courageous person I have ever met. This book is dedicated to my mother.

Chapter 1

Every person, on planet Earth, living or dead has had a perfectly good series of life events that has done nothing more than make us enjoy life, just to have it taken all away in one fell swoop. Hopefully anytime that happens, it is only a auto repair problem or kids going off to college; maybe a wife leaving you, or whatever it may be that forges a unexpected and disliked situation. But most of the times those events do not destroy a person. In the case of a spouse leaving, it does hurt a person for possibly years afterwards, so what could be worse? This question comes and goes so often in our lives that we may take the inquiry for granted.

Mary was asking that question herself. "What could be worse?" she asked herself, while she peered out the window. It was in the deep of night, and her daughters were asleep in their room, leaving her alone and cold by her window. "Why is it always raining when you feel bad?" The thought left her mind as she described to herself the events that led to this disheartened time and again in her mind, as if she had never heard the story before, and she found herself enraptured every time. She pondered her thoughts as if she had driven by a terrible car accident, and found herself unable to take her eyes away.

The images of her late husband of two years, the abusive boyfriend that followed, and an overwhelming feeling of helplessness crept into every thought and occupied every emotion, while she starred at the black, listless sky. The images would move through her mind, faster than she could count, but one image kept creeping back, and hurting her over and over, as if her mind was torturing itself on purpose. The image was that of her eldest daughter crying and crouched beside the wall with her hands on her bleeding face, and the force of the impact of his terrible blow moving through her little hands, and into her eyes.

The grief and guilt of the thought pounded from the inner reaches of her mind, and she could hardly slow them down. They came from a far distance and gained speed every moment, so as she stood at the window remembering an event from a matter of days before from another person's perspective, the pain wretched her body into a heave. She felt guilt that she never knew existed. From the pain in her stomach came nausea, and then her head would spin.

She sat down; still staring out at the gloomy evening and tears slowly rolled down her cheeks. But the image would not leave her alone. She remembered herself bleeding also from the eye, lip, and nose. She remembered pushing herself up from the ground, but the pain in her side nearly brought her back to cold floor. She couldn't hold in a breath, but in the corner of her eye, Mary could see the cowardly attack on her child and ignoring the pain, she stood and charged toward the man.

The pounding of the guilt came again and it gave her a headache this time. She could not stop the tears, and worse was her inability to let go her guilt of her child's beating as it ate at her spirit like worm at its meal. What kind of world allows people to be born with that much hatred, she would ask herself, but only more tears came from the thought. The images of her daughter selflessly taking the blows that were designed for her, crying and bleeding through her fingers as she held her head tight. The image of his booming hand that came with so much force that it broke three of her fingers would not leave. Again her mind screamed out, so that if she were a siren the entire world could hear her cry. But her lips were silent. The pain stopped her tongue, and as if it were doused with a poisonous hatred, it was left numb.

Mary took a moment on a different tone of thought. She remembered a time a couple months before. Last May, Emily was making images in construction paper, and cutting out pieces with her dull scissors. At one point, the young child cut out a flower and gave it to Mary. She could remember the child's sweet and innocent face with a large smile giving so freely to her mother. Mary's stomach churned and she could feel the pain of her situation.

Mary pondered more; the effect of her dwindling life in this place weighed on her mind. She knew her options well, but she had always been a strong person, and a retreat in the wake of disaster would prove to be the right choice, but to what end would it lead her? Could her pride be strong enough to solve her dilemma of money and jobless state, or would it falter and be the end of her and her beloved daughters? Mary was sure that the latter would be the most likely. Her mind ached from its argument with itself.

Mary could ask her mind to be silent, but it would refuse. She could ask her mind just to whisper and it would yell out her guilt. "Why do I feel guilty?" she whispered to herself. As she thought of the answer, she was amazed to see that her breath from her whisper fogged her window. The chill of the night air was boiling compared to that of the blood of her veins. This cold is not one of hatred, no, but more like a hollow cave where the only wind that traveled through would cut a person to the bone. "I feel guilty because I picked him. I feel guilty because I couldn't stop him fast enough!" she yelled in her mind.

Mary could not even grasp the idea, as a sigh of pain and suffering accompanied a tear of hopelessness onto her cheek. "Fine," she said to herself. "I'll go back."

Chapter 2

The Potato State was beginning its autumn release of leaves as she drove her station wagon into the small town of Lone City. Her father was one of the few lawyers in the town, as the population of Lone City found itself to be at only five thousand inhabitants. The red, orange, and yellow leaves on the trees made Mary smile as the slightly hilly roads lead her to the town. The sights of nature and familiarity could do no harm to her nerves. Michelle and Emily looked fondly upon their mother. They were happy to see their mother smiling for the first time in the two weeks since they were attacked, and it helped them to find serenity from the stormy weeks.

She passed through the main road of the town, but it seemed as if time had almost forgotten the town. The buildings seemed unchanged in the seven years since Mary had seen them, and the sight brought pleasure and ease to her mind. She drove down another mile or so, passed the center of town, and turned on a street named Canterbury Lane. The old homes passed slowly by but after a few minutes Mary found her home tucked gently behind a solitary giant elm. She parked on the street outside of a two-story off-white colored house with a few plants on the porch and green hedges surrounding the property, and opened the door of her car to reveal a new life.

She walked to the door with a suitcase in one arm and the hand of Emily in the other. Michelle followed behind them carrying her own little suitcase. Mary decided to knock since her pride from leaving seven years ago in such a rage and her guilt still seemed to fight her. Mary swallowed as the door opened, and her mother came forth. The familiar smell of the house had not changed from what Mary could remember, and the nostalgia that came rushing from the smell brought back good memories of her youth. She was happy to be home, but her anxiety was still great. It would take some time to get used to the circumstances that brought her to that house. At that moment, she was sure that the transition would be rocky at best.

"Oh, come in, come in," shouted her mother. "Oh, look at my little angels." She smiled and kissed both little girls on the cheek as they made their way into the house. Just to the left of the doorway was the staircase leading to the second level. It was marble and curved as it went up as to make a spiral as it climbed through the air. The stairs were wide, spanning five feet, making a full turn up to the next floor. The spiral array made for more room in the house and a stunning appearance to any person as they walked into the home. Mary's parents did not have bundles of money, but what they did have they had put towards the house in the last thirty years to make it a lovely home. But as Mary walked in being reminded of her youth, she knew that lovely was too much of an understatement as the walls illuminated the rooms with paintings and fixtures. Even the colors seemed to have been well thought out. There was little change from last she had seen of it, but she could hardly hold her balance in its wake.

Just after the three made their way in the hallway that was adjacent to the stairs, Mary's father

Daniel Stern came forth to see his daughter. At the same time "Nanny," as the children called her, was hugging her grandchildren without a ceasing moment, the same thought came to the now sixty year old man as put his arms around his daughter. The four girls quickly moved into the living room just a few feet from the hallway, and took a seat on the couches, while Mary's father made his way out to the car to bring in the suitcases and bags.

Mary was hosting a complexity of emotions and thoughts in her heart and mind respectively. She was happy to be home, but her parents' smiles were shredding her strength. She felt as though she might lose her mind. The term "killing them with kindness" was suddenly very real to the pride-filled woman. She realized, though, that the time with her parents was exactly what she needed whether she wanted to believe it or not. She knew that she needed to lose her pride and simply accept that a few tough problems in life had made her hit the ground, and a few helpful hands to lift her back up would not hurt.

The two young girls were excused to go up to their new room and unload their toys and await dinner. They played with their dolls up in their room as they always did. Mary and her parents took the opportunity and talked for a while in the late afternoon before her mother would go to make dinner. They talked about the town for a bit and different houses for rent in relatively pretty neighborhoods and how Mary's parents could pay the rent for just a few months until Mary could find a good job and get back on her feet. Mary swallowed the lump in her throat from having to rely on them and thought of her two daughters. From that moment on she would have to reluctantly accept their generosity.

For the time being she would stay there until she could find a place of her own. The memories of youth came back to Mary as she walked into her old room. The bed was made and it smelled a bit stuffy, as the door had been closed for a while. Luckily one of the windows was open, allowing fresh air to cascade in and Mary starred at the fabric blinds as they danced in the wind. Her mother had obviously changed the sheets and covers with the impending return of her daughter and had opened the window to let a breeze through the room. Surprisingly the air was not too cold even though the fall was moving in quickly. Mary walked over to the window and just starred out to the yard in the front of the house.

The green grass was well kept, just as it had always been. She would spend many hours as a child just gazing out of her window looking at the lonely elm tree that stood tall in the yard, only surrounded by grass. As a youth she would think of the future, or magnificent weddings, or a large house with a horse in the back yard running. But now her dreams were different. It was true that she still had visions of grandeur, but for now it was not a large house with a horse, but peace of mind. She was still nervous from the two weeks prior to her move, and she wanted to put it all behind her.

Mary was still thinking of her late husband and she worried about the transition for her daughters. It seemed as though she could not allow herself to stop worrying. She hoped that the schools here would do well for her older daughter. She wanted all of the benefits of a large city, but with the peace of a small town. Another worry weighed on her mind. She needed to find a job, and in such a small town it could be difficult to find something, but she knew one thing for certain. That one thing was that having her father help her find a job was out of the question. They had given her more than enough. They had given her not only financial help, but also her mother could watch over Emily as she worked and even could take care of both Michelle and Emily in the afternoon if Mary had to work late. These were enough charities for Mary for the time being, but the comfort of familiarity did allow her to unload a bit of her clothes to pass the time as she prepared a dress for the next day of job searching and placing her daughter in school.

She woke up the next morning to the sounds of her daughters downstairs talking with their grandmother, and to the familiar smell of breakfast that filled her room. She moved the heavy covers away from her torso and looked down at the embroidered flowers that hung on the fabric and remembered safe times at home when no problem could reach her. She looked around to see that her room was still the same lavender color that it had always been. The white chest of drawers was just two feet from the side of the bed, with a window above them and another across on the other wall facing the front yard.

She found her way to her feet looked over to see the digital clock on her bedside table reading seven forty-five. "Way to early to be awake," she thought to herself, though having children basically set up her life in a perpetual early wake up call. She laughed to herself as she thought of how children could find a way to be awake so early in the morning, *every* morning. Mary looked through the clothes that she had set out and found something for the day. She picked up a flowered dress, much like the flowers on her bedspread containing a mixture of Sunflowers and Lilies, and she smiled at the color scheme of the dress. It was a spring dress, light and bright, but she felt that light and bright was the path to better feelings for that particular day, and luckily the warm weather outside agreed.

Mary went to shower and wake herself for the day. The warm water was pleasing to her skin and nerves, as it was a way of putting off the day, a way to hang on to the peace of sleep and pleasant dreams. She finished her shower and dressed slowly, once again trying to put off the rest of the day. But before she could finish the thought, it seemed, she found herself downstairs at the table with her daughters smiling at her as they looked over their pancakes with great anticipation.

"When do I have to go back to school?" asked Michelle. But as quickly as she said it, Emily opened with, "I want to go to school."

Mary smiled at the both of them and looked back to her older child. "I am going today to enroll you at the schools here, so you can start tomorrow." A frown came over the little girl's face, but it was commonplace. All children had a dislike for school, all children it seemed but little Emily who had not yet had the opportunity of school. She looked at her mother with open eyes awaiting a response to her statement.

"And for you, Little Bit," said Mary. "You get to go to school next fall. So you just watch the leaves outside in the window. When they leave the trees and hit the ground and your grandfather cleans them up so that it can snow, and after it snows you see some flowers of every color. Then it will become hot and dry, and finally after that when the leaves are back on the trees and their colors are changing once more, then you can go to school." Mary paused for a second with a smile and waited for a response.

Emily was no fool and understood that it would be quite some time and that her mother was beating around the bush, but she was content for the moment with the anticipation of snow and smiled none the less. How could she not with a new stack of pancakes waiting for her as she looked back down?

Mary went back to her coffee, but she was stopped by Michelle's face. More than once in the last couple of weeks Mary would break down at the thought of her daughter when seeing her bruised eye, and the mark from her stitches, or her bundled hand. Mary could cry at the sight of her broken fingers alone. It was a painful world that they once had to endure. Mary could not help but to feel broken just the same.

The rest of the morning went by quickly and as the little girls went to watch some cartoons, Mary put on her makeup and tediously searched for the right shoes. She left the house and drove to the center of town. Although the town was small, corporations found it on a map and moved in. The town had a mall with couple major department stores, not that many people lived in the town, but it saw a generous portion of vacationers. Mary moved her attention to a Chili's restaurant. She had not had a job since high school that she kept for any length of time, and waiting tables still seemed to bring in the most money of any of her latest adventures. It was also a quick fix to her problems, as she needed money and a job quickly. She could always find time to find another; better job, but the urgency of today took its toll.

Before Mary made her way up the small flight of stairs just outside the restaurant a friendly and familiar voice raised up. "Mary," sounded the voice. "Mary!"

Upon turning around she saw the face of an old friend from high school named Pam. They were close then and it pained Mary to leave town while her friend ended up staying in the hometown due to her marriage.

"Hi Pam," shouted Mary. Mary was wrong to assume that the largest overflow of emotions for her day would be dealing with her parents and her pride. An unexpected friend made for a breach of her emotional security. Whether this would be a pleasant encounter was still dangling somewhere in the air.

"Hi, I didn't know that you were back in town?" questioned Pam.

"Yes, yes, I'm back in town."

"I'm so sorry about Gerard," started Pam again. "I wanted to come to St. Paul for the funeral, but my son Robert was having surgery at the time."

"Oh, it is all right," said Mary. "I was so bent out of shape that I couldn't even notice the people around me."

"Oh, you poor thing!" exclaimed Pam.

"Don't worry, don't worry. I'm better now, but I still miss him."

"Well, I'm sorry to hear it, but, are you in town for a vacation or what?"

"No, I moved back here for a bit. Hey, I want to tell you all about it, but right now I'm going to try and get a job. Would you like to come over to the house this afternoon?"

"I would love to! At your parents' place?" she questioned.

"Yes, yes. Oh, it is so good to see you," shouted Mary.

"Well, if you are looking for a job, I can get you started with this Mary Kay that I'm working with. But one way or the other, I won't keep you. I'll see you later."

"I can't wait," and with that comment Mary finally let off another good smile. They had become rare things, these true smiles, and it pleased Mary to find them again.

"I didn't expect that to go so well," Mary said aloud to herself turning back to her stairs.

Chapter 3

The hour in which her friend was to join her was quickly coming. She had applied with success at Chili's and luckily she would start immediately. After the reassurance of impending finances, she easily enrolled her daughter into school. It wouldn't take her long to get into a groove where she would be able to make reasonable money at her new job. In the meantime it was determined; not only by her father, but also by herself, to look for a better job. Nevertheless, the day seemed to be going well so far, and her old friend would make for an interesting evening later. It had been years since she had a decent heart-to-heart conversation with another woman beyond her mother's ever vigilant ear, and the anticipation moved up and down her spine. Although the nearing friendship loomed, Mary knew that she still needed to unwind more. Just as the trip and the comfort of home were slowly making her feel better, Pam could be a catalyst with the transition.

Near two o'clock a knock was heard throughout the house as Pam arrived. The delighted Mary, almost like a teenager, nearly ran to the door to let her friend in. The smiles on the two women's faces were not too different; both were large and each was happy to see the other.

Mary and Pam sat down in the living room. Michelle and Emily were causing a little bit of annoyance, but beyond some quick complaining they were trying to join in with the conversation as the two women explained the past years to each other. The two young daughters were involved and alive with the conversation until Mary's ex-boyfriend came up in the matter. The two girls didn't really know what to do, as they were both still uneasy about the matter. And to keep themselves far from that time in their recent lives, they decided to go outside and play.

"Oh don't worry about them," started Mary as she saw her friend noticing the girls' uneasiness. "They are still pretty upset. And I guess that I am as well."

"I'm so sorry that whole mess happened," responded Pam.

"Well, it is okay I guess. He is going to be in prison for a while, but for only fifteen months. What will happen when he gets back out of prison? I do not know, but I will not spend my life running from someone."

"I know what you mean. Maybe you should just stay here in town, or better yet, how about that witness protection program?" Pam said with a chuckle consisting of a mixture of playfulness with a hint of seriousness.

"Witness protection?" shouted Mary. "I will not spend my life in hiding. I might stay here for a while to get my mind off of it, but I don't need the government to hide me!"

"Well, I guess that you will do what you have to do to protect your family, but who knows, maybe they could get you a nice condo in Beverly Hills or something!" The two laughed the thought of the high life with warm weather.

"I know," Mary started again. "They are all that matter to me now." Mary's eyes and mind wandered away from the conversation at that moment, and towards the window where she could see Emily and Michelle playing in the yard; running after each other with nothing but enjoyment radiating from their youthful spirits. She was thinking of different times when the girls were just a bit younger and her husband was still alive, and her problems were so far away. But it ended just as abruptly as it had started, and Mary's small time in her own personal oasis was over.

The two talked and talked, until the sun went down and dinner was prepared, and then they talked throughout dinner, and late into the night. Mary tucked in her two daughters who seemed to sleep better away from St. Paul, while still talking to her friend. But that did not stop them, the two talked until one in the morning. Pam left and Mary was filled with joy that her friendship was building again. Mary decided to go to bed, but once again a pure and true smile came to her face. She felt as if there was hope once more in her life. She was home, and in the short thirty hours or so that she had been there, she was letting go of her pride and enjoying her parents help. She was happy to have a friendly ear to talk with, and a job to support her family. The next day was to be the first step in her new life. Mary would take Michelle to school, search for a place to stay, and then go to work. Her life seemed to be perking up, "Thank you God. Thank you God. Thank you God," Mary kept saying in her head. "Thank you God. Thank you God. Thank you God." And until she found sleep, "Thank you God."

The morning came soon, and the alarm clock resonated with what Mary could only imagine to be Hell's bells. Mary had the idea that she was to get up before her daughter at the early hour of six thirty, but to her surprise, the two girls were awake already. She understood that they were early risers, but this was beginning to get ridiculous!

Mary took her opportunity as an early riser on that morning and found her way to the shower. She once again put off the day, for just a bit of time, and remembered jubilant times of her youth. She remembered the moment that she took Michelle home from the hospital to meet the world for the first time, and she remembered her wedding. A smile came to her face, and she nearly broke down into tears of joy. She was becoming more and more attached to these morning showers. She normally took her showers in the evening, but this seemed to be a better wake up than coffee could ever provide, but better still it offered her peace of mind.

Michelle got ready, and in time, the two left for school. Mary was happy that their lives were back into some type of rhythm. She smiled and kissed her daughter as she left to go sprinting into the playground to find new friends. Michelle was not shy when it came to other children. Her heart was filled with joy. She ran with her little dress on, maybe for the last time before it began to get cold every day, and headed towards the crowd of children her size. Mary simply looked on as the world was still, and enjoyed the sight of her older daughter. She could realize the vastness of her world, but it was the simplicity of the life she worked for.

Mary proceeded from there to look at a duplex that she had found in the classified section of the newspaper. The place was not very large, but that did not matter. She didn't mind one bathroom either, the three of them found ways to share pretty easily.

She was pleased and the price range would be well enough for now, although her father would insist on paying for the rent for at least the first month so that she could get settled down. Mary felt that fighting them about finances would get her nowhere, although she never liked it when her parents made it easy on her. She wanted to feel independent again, and even for this brief time that she had stayed with her parents, she could feel that autonomy slipping away, although her feelings of it were much exaggerated.

Mary finished her chore for the day and went home to change clothes for her job. She was given a Chili's shirt for her to wear and she was to supply the blue jeans. The uniform was simple, and hopefully the job would be as well. The only time that she had spent waiting tables during her youth and at a little restaurant in town that never got very busy. She could only imagine the complexity that this job would hold over her, but it was that complexity that would help to sustain her children, so she swallowed the ostensibly ever-present lump in her throat and continued on.

Mary found her way to the entrance of the restaurant and she walked in for her first day. Four o'clock rang and she could smell fajitas as she moved past the doorway. The pleasant scent made her smile and, for a brief moment, made her hungry. She was greeted by the same manager that she met the day before and without much talk, he put her to work in a small section of the restaurant, giving her only two tables so that she could get herself aquatinted with the servicing of others. Her section was not to be seated for another half-hour, so in the thirty minutes a fellow employee went along with her showing her the restaurant and the computer system that she would use to order the food.

Mary took in as much as she could, but she felt overwhelmed by the amount of information. She was worried that she might not succeed at this new job, and hoping that she would find a better job soon, but she remembered the two small little faces that she worked for and her energies were refilled.

Mary spent her first night running back and forth trying to learn the drinks from the bar, and trying to find dishes and condiments. Although she didn't have many customers, she was not prepared for the pandemonium of the restaurant business. At a couple of times during her trauma she felt like quitting, but just as always, those same two faces gave her strength. There are no words in the human vocabulary to capture the feeling she had for her children, not only then when she needed their love the most, but at all times. She loved them more than air, and nothing brought her more happiness, or sorrow, than her children.

Mary finished her night, and headed home. It was just after midnight when she opened the front door. The house was dark, but warm and comforting. One light in the kitchen was left on and a light at the top of the stairs. Mary turned off the light in the kitchen and then proceeded up the stairs. She turned off the stair light and felt her way to her room, moving her feet at little steps and her hands pressed up against the rough wall. She turned on the light there, and looked for her nightgown. Mary went quickly, after changing, to Michelle and Emily's room. She slowly, and hopefully silently, opened the door to peer into the room. She could see her babies' faces with the covers pulled up to their chins. They slept in the same manner. Both were bundled up like a burrito in their covers. Mary was lost in the moment, in the same manner as earlier in the day when she watched Michelle run and play. Staring at her peaceful children made her instantly feel more at peace in her own mind and troubles. But instead of momentary happiness that she had been finding lately, this felt deeper and stronger, and a sense of optimism forged its way into her mind and spirit. Mary had hope for the first time in two years. She promised herself at that moment not to run from job to job, and more importantly, not from guy to guy either. She didn't need them anymore. All she needed was bundled up in a couple small packages of joy. She felt sad that she didn't get to hear about Michelle's first day of school, but she would get up early in the morning to find out. Mary took another look at her babies and then closed the door silently and went to bed. Sleep came quickly to the tired mother, and before she knew it, she was just as peaceful as anyone in the house was.

The morning came quickly, but luckily for Mary it was a Saturday. Mary opened her eyes slowly, blinking away the sleep, and hearing her daughters downstairs. She quickly jumped up to take a shower. She had to be at work at eleven, but that would leave her with more than enough time to talk with her family.

The shower was a good sanctuary as it normally was, but Mary could feel the last few days, lack of rest, in her body. She was growing tired, but that did not matter. She was anxious to hear about her daughter's first day at a new school, and she was anxious to try again at her new job. Mary was determined to accomplish all that she had set out to do. She had always been a responsible person, and always a hard worker. Mary was the type of person who would go for what she needed and damn anyone who would stand in the way of her responsibilities.

Mary made her way downstairs to see her daughters watching early morning cartoons, and eating some scrambled eggs while lying on the floor, still in their pajamas; Michelle in pink and Emily in bright blue.

"Would you like some eggs, dear?" asked her mother as Mary moved into the kitchen.

"Yes, please. Oh, I need some coffee," Mary said smiling. She poured herself a cup of coffee and walked over to her daughters.

"How was your first day of school yesterday, Michelle?"

"It was fun, Mommy. We got to spend a whole hour outside during lunch and recess. It was great!"

Mary smiled and chatted with her children as they had some breakfast. The same sense of serenity that she found last time made its way to her again in the morning. Her children were the only things to her; her ambrosia really, and her will to carry on. Mary sat with them as long as possible, and then succumbed to the clock and dressed herself for work.

Just before Mary was to go to work her friend Pam called.

"Hey Mary," said Pam as Mary answered the phone.

"Hi, how are you doing?"

"I'm doing great. Hey, I'm taking Robert to the park a little later, I was wondering if you and the girls would like to join us?"

"Well I would love to, unfortunately I have to go to work."

"Well that is no problem," explained Pam. "I can still take the girls with me if they would like to go."

"That sounds great, and I don't even have to ask them, I'm sure that they would love to go with you, but Emily can be a handful. Are you sure that you want to?"

"Oh, I'm sure she won't be much of a problem. She is such a sweet angel."

Mary smiled at the thought, but knew otherwise. She loved her daughters and they were great almost always, but when they were bad, they were really bad. "Well, if you don't mind, they need to get out and play anyway. They spend so much time in front of the television!"

"Great! Well I'll pick them up a little after noon then."

"Okay, thanks Pam, I'll see you soon."

Mary was glad that she had a friend and that the girls would have somewhere to go to have fun so quickly after moving. Mary went over to her daughters, who were still watching cartoons, and said, "Girls, later Pam is going to come by and take you to the park, okay?"

"But Mommy," cried Emily. "I want you to take us to the park."

Mary went over and bent down on her knees and hugged her daughter. "I can't today, but as soon as I have a day off we will go, and we will do it soon, before it gets too chilly."

The appeased child smiled and went back to her cartoons. Mary felt herself lucky to have such happy children. After all that they had been through, they seemed as calm as anyone could. They had an unusual amount of joy and it was somewhat bewildering to Mary at times, but she thanked God for the young girls' constant jubilation.

Chapter 4

Work, on the other hand, presented no situation to smile about. Mary still had a small section, but she was still learning everything, and her feet were beginning to hurt as she walked speedily from point to point. But a small ray of light came in near one o'clock as her parents came through the front door. "Maybe they came to eat," she said to herself.

Mary walked to the front door, but before she could say anything, her mother grabbed her by the arms and said, "Hurry, we have to go to the hospital, there has been an accident!"

"An accident," screamed Mary. "What kind of accident?"

"A car accident," said her father. "The girls are hurt, we have to hurry. The car is parked out front. Lets go now!"

Mary did not need the time to wait and see if her boss would mind. She didn't care. The worst nightmare that any mother could have was happening right then and there. She had nothing else in mind as they ran out to the car. That ray of hope that she had been nursing in the last twenty-four hours diminished and a powerful anxiety took its place on Mary's fragile psyche.

The three were silent as Mary's father drove quickly to the hospital. Although it was only a five-minute trip, the time seemed like an eternity to Mary. She couldn't even think of what could have happened or how or why. All she knew is that her daughters were in trouble. Mary couldn't hear anything, not even as her dad laid on the horn to clear the way. She was completely without sense of the happenings around her. The only thought that could find its way into her mind was: "God, please let them be all right." The buildings and street signs moved by in a blur. Even objects directly in front of her became cloudy and unrecognizable.

Mary's father drove right up to the emergency entrance, and Mary and her mother jumped out and ran inside. Mary was directed to a waiting room, but she could not wait. She ran through the halls looking for the rooms. She found the room where Emily was. Mary peered into the room to see more than six doctors, in blue coats, working on her little girl. All she could see is her little feet and part of her arm sticking out of the bodies of blue. Her body was burgundy red as her blood was drying on her skin. Before she could even realize what was happening, an instrument with an overwhelming reputation came into her sight. Even the smallest child recognizes a defibrillator from seeing it on television. Mary watched in terror as a doctor placed the paddles on the girl and her little form jumped as the electricity surged through her delicate body.

As the girl's boded spasms with the electricity Mary let out an uncontrollable scream. Another shock moved through the child's body, and as if Mary and Emily were connected, the shock forced the little girl's body to jump, and again at the same instant, Mary burst into yet more tears, and uninhibited screams. Her father and mother were trying to hold her as she began to lose control of her feet and legs. Another jolt and another wail by Mary commenced just moments later.

And, as it seemed, before Mary could even have another thought they were shocking Emily again, and more tears ran down her cheeks. She couldn't even imagine what was happening. Her world was falling apart with every jolt. After two more attempts the doctors stopped their efforts, and the masked man holding the paddles let his head drop, almost as if it would have fallen off without his neck.

"No! Don't stop!" screamed Mary pounding on the doors to the room while a nurse frantically held the doors shut. "No! No! No!"

Before the moment could sink in, she thought again. "What about Michelle!" she screamed again. She turned to a doctor near her, and in a moment of agony and despair she could see him shake his head. She had lost both things that had any value to her, and she collapsed and hit the floor. The rest of the hospital looked on as she screamed and cried in agony. Her mind could not comprehend all that had happened. All she wanted to do was cry and so she did. Her tears did not stop, even as her father pulled her away and into a chair and held her tight, she just cried. The rest of the afternoon, the evening, all night, and into the next morning Mary did not think; she only cried.

She awoke the next morning from a nightmare. And then she opened her eyes to realize that her real life was worse than the nightmare and she began to cry again. She was moved while she slept and found herself on a couch in her parent's house, but it mattered not where she was. She only wanted to cry, because everything seemed unimportant. "Everything is gone; so of course nothing is important," her monologue screamed back at itself. She felt hunger, but it only lasted for a moment before her mind was plagued with smiles from her daughters and the sights, in her mind, of her little Emily dying on the table, her limp body jumping with pulses. She still didn't even know how it had happened. "What the Hell has been let loose upon my world," her mind raced.

Noon came quickly and Mary's home was soon filled with people she had never known, and did not care to meet now. They tried to offer kind words, but Mary gave them no response. Each time a person would come and try to comfort her they were given no word while she stared off into the distant wall; unwavering in her mystification, and Mary's mother would have to tell them that she couldn't talk then. It was a daunting task for the grandmother for it hurt her as well to lose her grandchildren.

During all of the kind words that did not matter to Mary, her father brought a bowl of soup, set it down on the coffee table, and looked into his daughter's eyes. His were hollow, tired and weary, but as he peered into her eyes, one could see that he was a pillar of light and joy in comparison. Mary's eyes did not just seem to be hollow, but there was no life in them at all. They didn't move as he talked to her. She didn't blink as she just stared off into the wall. Her head would move about here and there, but her eyes were in a straight line. Her body was lifeless. Her father left her line of sight, and still no movement, and as quickly as her life had become livable again, it crashed and went deeper towards the caverns of torment than ever.

The next few days up until the funeral revealed no change in Mary's demeanor. Mary did not shower and only ate two meals in three days. Mary hardly slept. She spent most of her time sitting on the couch, or in her room gazing at a picture of her late husband and her two daughters in a daze. The photo was taken just a few months before his death and the children were alive with happiness. Her reasons for living had left her. "How can I go on. I'm nothing without them," she said to herself again and again. She spent hours crying looking at the same photograph, remembering good times and only good times. She was suffering more than she could ever imagine anyone could suffer. She felt nauseous most of the day, but she gathered herself with hardship to prepare for the funeral.

She was hardly able to hold herself together even to shower and get dressed. The warm water droplets from the shower did not have the same feeling as they did just four days prior. Now their temperature felt cold as ice, as if she were being tortured in a hailstorm. She didn't care though. It didn't even matter if she froze to death in the shower. It could not bring back those things that she needed. She needed her children, and now she was stuck with nothing. She dressed herself, but needed her father to hold on to as she walked to the car and to the church. She made no noise, no comment, and no sign of coherence. Much of her wanted to die that morning and a freezing death in the shower, or perhaps a heart attack, or even a damned meteorite might have been better than trying to comprehend going to a funeral.

They reached the church, and she just sobbed. The last twenty-four hours had seen fewer tears than the first day of her misery, but her pain took its form in other ways, including her many hours of staring at the wall, and what seemed to be coming into play as a yelling bout with her own mind. "This could not be happening to me! What have I ever done to deserve this? I was sinful! No I wasn't! Then why am I here?" she screamed in her mind and then silenced, but for only a moment.

"How did all of this happen," she thought to herself. "Why was Pam hit by a truck, with my two little ones in the back? Why would God do that to me? Why am I still here, and why can't I trade places with them? No matter though. I will die soon enough. I can't even imagine a reason to stay alive. My life is over." She looked on as the priest spoke kind words and she imagined that this were her funeral as well. She could see three caskets up in the front as she pictured the dreadful imagine in her mind.

She walked outside for the burial and the leaves were blowing off of the trees and collecting on the ground. It was cold and cloudy outside. It almost looked as though it would rain or snow on them, which would be fitting burial weather, but it did not. It didn't matter to Mary though. They were trivial matters; soon forgotten.

Chapter 5

In the following weeks she had cried a little less as each day passed. It moved from a steady cry all day long into hour-long bouts four or five times a day. To the naked eye it would look as though she was feeling better. But the war that raged inside of her mind and heart was far worse than it seemed. She could not get the pictures of her daughters dying out of her head. They invaded her during the day and even worse in her dreams at night. The few times that she would find rest and allow herself sleep; she would wake up at least, twice a night with nightmares. She couldn't stay focused on any task at hand. Her mother tried to get her to sit with her and sew a little bit and try to focus on something, but with only a few minutes into the task, Mary hung her head down and did not wish to bring it back up. Many times, she would retreat back to her room and stay there for hours.

Mary's parents did not know what to do with her. Clearly she was dying inside. The pastor of their church had visited twice a week for the last two weeks, and Mary's parents kept asking him to come more and more.

Another month passed, and Mary's lethargic attitude did not change. Now she seemed to get angry from time to time without provocation. She was not working, and she was staying at home, so she had no pressures. It almost seemed as though she was forcing problems into her life. She spent hours up in her room pacing and talking to herself while hiding bouts of arguments with God. She would fight with her own thoughts and then with God. Sometimes her screams could be heard from outside the house, and many passing walkers became worried to the point of fearing for their own safety after hearing the terrorizing screams.

"Why did you take them away from me? What do you want from me?" she would say to God. "Have I sinned in some way to force this Hell upon me? My husband died, and then you took my children. What do I have left for you to take? Nothing! Just take me now, just take me," and even more quietly, "just take me." And at the end of every episode like this, she would collapse to her knees and cry. With her face in her hands she ended her arguments with God every day. No amount of crying or prayer would make her feel better and every morning with tear filled eyes asking God to take her life.

One morning about a week later she woke up in her bed. She looked out the window. She was still snuggled up in her bed, with her toes just a little chilly from the cold weather now in town. It would be November soon, and Lone City was now in the thirty-degree temperature every day. She looked out to see the buds where the leaves were on the branches of her favorite elm. She looked at the tree with its lifeless limbs and thought to herself. She was now just like the tree. She was nothing more than a dead standing piece of would-be life, with all of the pieces that make it bright and cheery and worthwhile gone. And just as the wind sucked away the leaves from the elm, the winds of life had taken her leaves away too. And with these thoughts of the world, her life, and her world as a whole, Mary decided not to get out of bed.

Mary wasn't intending on staying in bed all day, but before long it was noon, and then it was the afternoon, and then evening was on its way, and Mary just lied in bed looking at her lonely favorite tree. She napped from time to time that day, but her eyes peered towards the tree for hours at a time. It was the type of stare that would frighten a man if he so much as glimpsed at it. It was the type of stare that could burn down a hillside, but it was not an angry look. It was the blank motionless force that gave it strength. More than a few times, her mother came in and asked her what was wrong and why she wouldn't get out of bed. Mary, knowing that her depression was becoming a burden on her mother and father, decided to lie and say that her stomach didn't feel well and she just wanted to stay in bed. For lunch her mother brought her some light soup and some Gatorade, but Mary didn't touch it. For dinner, her mother did the same thing. Mary had, by then, gained some appetite and ate the dinner, but didn't decide to get out of bed.

She told herself that she was just tired of thinking, pacing and mourning, and that a day off would do her good. She told herself that the next day she would get up and move around and maybe go visit her daughters' graves. She knew that it would make her cry, but she couldn't just stay in bed forever. Mary told herself to do these things.

The next morning came, and Mary just looked out and saw the tree and decided that she did not want to get up that day either. It was so easy to give up, and Mary decided just to give in. She spent a few hours happy with her decision, it felt good to lay in bed and relaxes, but after some time went she remembered the promises to herself.

"God," she yelled at herself. "You just sat there and told yourself, promised yourself, that you were going to get up and do something, and now look at you!" she continued. "You are a waste of life and human energy. You can't even keep the promises that you make to yourself, and you are a burden to your parents. Why can't you stay with the goals that you set out for yourself?" she screamed in her head, still talking to herself as if her mind was a different entity. "So here we are, and you know what? It is your fault. Yes, that's right, your fault. Your children would not be dead if it wasn't for you!" she now sat up in bed and began to tell herself out loud. "Yes! If you didn't have to go to work that day then you could have been with them, maybe you would have gone at a different time or something. Anything! Or better yet, if you didn't have to move back here then it wouldn't have happened at all! You have destroyed your own life due to your incompetence," she began to tell her self, not only out loud but also in a louder voice. "If you didn't make the damned decision to quit your job and date that piece of crap man that attacked you, then you wouldn't be afraid of St. Paul, and you would not be here. Not only that, but you skimped out on school when you were younger! If you had just spent more time in school then you wouldn't have to worry about a job, or worry about a boyfriend, or worry about anything, but look at what you have done to your life. You are a disgrace! It probably did your children well when they died. They didn't have to deal with your failure as a mother anymore!"

Her monologue started to get loud and her parents went quickly up the stairs to see whom she was talking to, but they both knew whom it was that she spoke to. Although they prayed in their hearts as they moved speedily up the stairs that they were wrong, their logic would prove to be victorious in the end. As the door swung open, their bad dreams had come alive as they watched her daughter slap herself in the face and bury her head in her hands, crying out with loud moan.

"Why have you destroyed your life, and why did you destroy theirs while they were still alive?" she questioned herself. "It is better that they are gone; you can't hurt them anymore," and the tears started. "You can't hurt them anymore," she murmured as she broke down in more tears.

Her mother ran over to her and put her hand on her shoulder and moved her hair out of her face, "It is okay," she said. "Shhhhh, it is okay." Mary's mother just looked over at her husband, and the two looked at each other. They didn't know what to do, and they didn't know how to deal with this. Mary barely noticed that her parents were there, so she just cried into the pillow.

Mary became increasingly angry with herself and spent even more time in her room. She was not just in bed now, though. She would pace back and forth, blaming herself for what happened in her life. After just another three days, her parents could not allow it to happen anymore and set up a series of visits to different psychologists and psychiatrists in Lone City. There were only a few, but Mary's parents were determined to find help for their daughter. In retrospect, they wished their epiphany had come sooner.

Mary wasn't sure what was happening when they walked her out of her room and towards the bathroom. She fought with them for just a bit in her sleepy stupor, but succumbed to their forces and went inside. Her father left as Mary's mother almost had to tear her clothes off to get her into the shower. This was the first time that she had been in the shower in two weeks. Mary didn't want to argue with her mother anymore and decided to simply wash herself. "Why are they doing this though?" she thought. She had heard them talking earlier. Were they going to take her somewhere? Maybe they were going to take her to the crazy house? "Well, I belong there," she thought.

Although she was against the idea of feeling good since her children died, she enjoyed the time under the warm pellets of water. They didn't feel warm the last time that she was in the shower, but it felt better this time. Mary thought for a moment and thought that the water must have felt better since she hadn't been in a shower in a while, but she knew that she wasn't feeling any better. She finished and began to get dressed with a set of clothes already put out for her. "Why am I wearing this?" she asked herself as she looked down at the suit. It was a dress outfit. "I must be going somewhere, and definitely not the crazy house like this." Mary thought about not getting dressed but she could hear that her mother was still right outside, and arguing was not the first item on her agenda for that day.

Mary reluctantly and slowly dressed herself, but finally walked out of the bathroom. She looked out to see her mother standing in the hallway near the stairs waiting for her daughter and Mary noticed that she was dressed up as well. Mary took more notice to her mother and found her to be wearing pearl earrings. "Where am I going?" she thought to herself. And with a few more moments of thought she could take it no longer. "Where are we going?" Mary asked her mother.

"We are going to see some doctors today, okay?"

"Doctors?"

"Yes, just some doctors. Therapists, actually," began her mother, but Mary quickly looked down in unhappiness. "No, no, no, don't worry, dear. If you don't like one then we will just go to another, don't worry. If you don't like any one of them, then you do not have to go to any therapist at all. It will be your decision. We just want to give you a couple of options."

"Okay," agreed Mary. She did not want to fight them, but she did not like this idea. She made the choice with the fewest aggravations for the moment, and that was the best she could do then.

They walked out to the car, and as they went out the front door Mary was hit hard by the cold air outside of the house. She had been inside for so long that she didn't notice the temperature change as severe as it had been. She looked up to see the sun glowing brightly with no cloud in the sky. She pondered how it could be so cold as the sun shone down on them without the blockage of anything in the air. She shivered even in her coat and got into the car. She spent the drive thinking of her children while her heavy heart stopped any emancipation of happy thoughts. Mary had stopped herself from crying most of the time now, but it fooled no one, as her depression seemed to be growing exponentially by the day. She felt like a person trying to dig herself out of a hole, and every scoop of dirt she moved away called for a wheelbarrow-full more to be put on top.

The first therapist's office of the day was large with a secretary and a few red chairs sitting in a hallway. Mary's father went and talked with the secretary as Mary fixated her eyes on the wall. She looked intently on the small little bumps in the wall and didn't focus on any of the words any person said, but simply on the wall. In a few moments the three found themselves in an office of a psychiatrist and Mary's parents explained the situation to the doctor. After chatting for a few minutes the doctor got into explaining his therapy.

"Well first we should put her on an anti-depressant drug to get her in a more malleable position, and then using psychotherapy we can find the unconscious problem, either in her past or recently, that has caused this depression."

"Well, we know the problem," started her father. "Her children passed away," he said in a whisper.

"Well, there still might be some other unanswered trauma that we need to solve," said the psychiatrist.

"Her husband died a few years ago also," explained Mary's mother, also in a whisper.

"I can still hear you," explained Mary, but she didn't care too much, as she found many things in the office to stare at and focus her thoughts.

"Well, there might be more problems, maybe with her childhood, that could be causing other problems."

"Her childhood," yelled Mary's father. "You want to put her on drugs and then worry about her childhood, when the problem is so apparent?"

"Many times there are other aspects in play," explained the psychiatrist.

Mary's father was somewhat angered by the entire situation, but before he could burst from this man's looking down at his child as a project instead of a person, his wife took control. "Well, we are going to go to a few other people and we will get back with you," she explained.

"Very well," said the psychiatrist.

It was not hard to see that Mary's parents were not very interested in this man, although they were quite intrigued at his techniques and how he could still be in business. His chilling and unsentimental description of his treatment sent shivers down her parents' spines.

The rest of the day didn't go with any more delight to Mary or her parents as they found more and more therapist pushing drugs and strange therapies that they didn't understand. Mary, although not unhappy with any of the doctors since she wasn't paying any attention to them, was becoming bored. She starred out the window as they headed for the last stop of the day. Her mind could not take control of a single thought and dwell on it, but it moved rapidly from thoughts with no apparent consistency or sequence, except for the undeniably negative underlining.

They walked into the office of the last psychologist for the day, and found that there was no secretary. However, the psychologist's door was open and they could see inside. The man was wearing a dark suit and tie and was standing; reading from a folder.

"Excuse me, doctor," announced Mary's father.

"Oh, hi," he responded with a large smile on his face. "Please come and have a seat."

The three started on their way, and the doctor moved some chairs together for them to sit.

"Your name is Doctor Ross, correct?" asked Mary's mother.

"Yes. I have already met your husband, but I have yet to meet your daughter," he said as he reached his hand to Mary with his eyes on her. She wasn't paying attention, and didn't even realize that he was talking to her, since none of the other doctors paid much attention to her she didn't expect his hand to be pointed in her direction.

"M-M-Mary," she said, not ready.

"Hello. It is nice to meet you. How are you feeling today?" he asked her.

"I'm sad," she replied while moving her head away. She wondered why he would ask a question with such an obvious answer.

"I see," he responded.

"It has been about two months since her children passed, and her depression has been getting worse and worse by the day," explained Mary's mother.

Doctor Ross turned to Mary. "Worse every day Mary?" he asked her.

Mary was startled. Why was he talking to her? Wasn't he trying to find out information from her parents? "I don't know. I just know that I have been sad since they left me."

"I see. Have you been tired lately?"

"Yes."

"Is it hard to get out of bed sometimes?" he asked.

"Every time," she responded coldly.

"Do you want to put her on any medication," interrupted Mary's father.

"No, normally I don't like to deal with medication. But if that is what you are looking for, I'm sure that there are a few therapists in town that can help."

"No, no! We have been to all of those other guys and they all want to put her on pills. They say that some of the side effects are drowsiness, and she can hardly get out of bed anyway."

Doctor Ross smiled. "I have always believed that medication should be left for those who have gone beyond our realm of thinking. Almost all depression can be solved without medication of any kind, but many people, especially in this country, want the quick fix. Too bad it doesn't really fix anything. My therapy is more involved with finding thinking patterns that lead to negative feelings and teaching positive patterns, that in turn, lead to positive thinking."

"That is good," replied Mary's father. "I think that is just what we are looking for. We haven't found much compassion today. I think you have the right idea. Well, we don't want to take up any more of your time Doctor, but thank you."

"Oh, don't worry. I have all the time that you need. I put away a lot of my afternoon for this, so don't feel rushed."

"Oh, that is kind of you, but I think we should head back," began Mary's mother. "We have been out all day, and I know that Mary would like to get home."

"All right," said Ross. The doctor looked Mary right in the eyes as she turned her head toward him. "Have a good day, Mary." He said it with such a stern but almost loving tone that it took Mary by surprise. It was easy to see that the Doctor was confident with himself, but what surprised Mary was the honest feeling that seemed to back each word that came from him. Mary also felt somewhat special, almost like his words carried no condescending thoughts, and she could sense his empathy with just a look into his face. He didn't make her feel like a number.

Mary's father shook the doctor's hand and nodded his head. "We might just be back," he said.

"Until then," replied the doctor with ease.

Chapter 6

The family left, and it would be easy to any spectator to see that Mary's parents liked this guy. They just didn't want to push Mary into anything. They helped her into the car and the three were silent for most of the trip home, but just before they got home, Mary's mother could wait no longer.

"Well, were there any of those guys that you liked?"

"I don't like the idea of therapy," explained Mary.

"Let's just say that if you did like the idea, which of them would you like?"

"Doctor Ross was the only one that talked to me, and looked at me."

"Would you like to just give it a try once? If you don't like the therapy, then you don't have to go back."

"Okay," said Mary without emotion. She still wasn't sure exactly what she wanted to do though. She wanted to feel better, but she had never been sure about shrinks. She was frightened that he would tell her that she was crazy. "I just might be," she thought to herself. "I did kill my own children. Maybe I am crazy. What if he can't help me? Will I be trapped in this forever? What if he tells me that I am a bad person? I've earned it, I guess. I'm scared. I'm tired. I want to sleep."

Mary went up to her room immediately after getting home. Her mother said something about making some dinner and setting up a time for her to meet up with the doctor again. Mary wasn't paying any attention, as all of her focus was to get back to her room. She had been out all day, being examined by doctors who all probably thought she was crazy. All she wanted to do was get in bed and forget that the day ever happened. She got undressed and laid in her bed under her covers. Mary felt hungry, but she also felt tired. She wasn't sure whether or not she was going to eat, but it didn't really matter to her one way or the other. It couldn't bring back her children, which was the only substance she had ever needed to ease any desires, including those extinguished with food.

Mary closed her eyes, and filled her heads with her negative thoughts that plagued her. She couldn't think of one happy moment that she ever had with her late husband or with her children. She could only think of the three dying and leaving her alone in life with no one to take care of her, but more importantly, no one for her to take care of. Mary cried a few tears, then felt the cool, soft pillow up against her head and let a tear leave her cheek - and then fell asleep.

Mary woke up and could smell the death of her family in the air. She was still blaming herself for the death of her children, and several times had found a way to blame the death of her husband on herself also. It was Tuesday that morning. She woke up to see an overcast day, unlike yesterday, and she could feel the cool air as she touched the window. She was able to get out of bed though, the first proactive step towards her recovery, and she didn't even know it. She stood by the window looking at her favorite, dead-looking elm, and once again it reminded her of her own life.

She was having trouble lately remembering happy times. As much as she tried, and as much as her parents urged her to think happy thoughts, her loss would not leave he mind.

Mary continuously thought that she could not live without them, how could she? The love of her family is what made her survive up until that moment, so what was she to do without her family? She didn't have their love anymore, and she had nothing to love. She had nothing to live for, and it was her own fault. Mary fought with herself with these thoughts in her head as she debated suicide. Her father kept a gun downstairs on top of the refrigerator, and she contemplated using it. It would end this horrible life she had known. She felt that she had only faced opposition throughout her life, and maybe ending it would be easier. "If I died, it would be easier on my parents," she thought to herself. Mary found herself to be a burden. They were being forced to take care of her needs, give her room and board, and now to pay for a psychologist. It would be easier to end it, she kept thinking.

Mary spent all morning looking at the tree and thinking how much easier it would be on her parents if she were gone. She shivered in her nightgown for at least an hour before she decided to put on clothes. But the comfort of warmth from the clothes did not help her demeanor. She felt just as bad as ever and her thoughts screamed of how she didn't deserve comfort. Why should she be happy when her children had suffered, and her parents had to suffer for her actions? Mary was angry with herself for the trouble that she was causing. She took her left hand and pressed her nails from her right fingers into the palm of her hand, to the point where she could see some blood. She cried from the pain and the abuse that she gave herself in her own mind. As she dug her fingers into her hand, Mary could think of nothing but how she didn't deserve happiness or safety, but only pain. After a moment longer, she could take no more. So with tears in her eyes, she sat down on her bed, holding her damaged limb and contemplated in more detail her death by suicide. The tears would fall, just like every other day. This endless stream of pain would fill a lake if only it was captured.

Mary's mother brought up some food for her for lunch, just as every other day for the last month. Mary watched as her mother moved into the room. She was not smiling. It had been a while since she had smiled. Mary immediately thought that since her mother was not happy, it was her fault, because of the burden that she was causing. Mary was silent as her mother placed the food down, kissed Mary on the top of the head, and left. Mary was begging to believe more and more that she was the cause of her mother's turmoil. "Look at her face," Mary said to herself. "She hates me! I'm stopping her from being happy." She needed to remove herself from their problems. She needed to leave.

Hours later, after dinner had passed, nightfall found its way to the little town of Idaho. Mary waited as her parents to go sleep. More than two hours after she could no longer hear them, she walked downstairs. Mary was not afraid of what she had to do. She needed to preserve her parents' lives, and although she had her first therapy session tomorrow, she was sure that the man wouldn't mind an extra hour off. Mary walked into the kitchen and took a chair with her. She trembled as she placed the chair at the bottom of the refrigerator and stood on it. Mary looked on top of the refrigerator and found the small six-barreled handgun. She took hold of the weapon, stepped down from the chair, and opened the barrel to see that it was loaded with three rounds. She rolled the wheel over to the middle bullet and lost a tear. Mary cocked the gun and put it to her head with her body nearly convulsing from its frightened shakes. Her mind was filled with so many thoughts and she could hardly even react to them all.

"I am doing this to mitigate their troubles," she thought to herself, thinking of her parents.

"But I don't want to die."

"Coward, you would rather hurt them, then end this whole problem?"

"But I don't want to die. I'm frightened."

"You are a burden! You killed your children, and you couldn't save your husband! You have failed them."

"But I'm afraid. Won't I go to Hell?"

"You deserve Hell for your actions. Do it! Plus, it can't be as bad as this. You are hurting your parents, end this! You are a murderer and you do not deserve to live. This is the death penalty. Solve this problem!"

"I can't. I'm afraid."

With that Mary released the hammer of the gun and put it back on top of the refrigerator and began to weep; her body was still with multiple spasms. After a few minutes of her emotional discharge, she feared that her parents would hear and come down to see her sitting shamefully in the kitchen. Mary walked back upstairs and cried herself to sleep thinking that maybe tomorrow God would let her die and let her go to Heaven and release her from her living Hell. She cried into her pillow and for a brief moment hoped for luck tomorrow with the therapist. But then she remembered that she didn't want herself to be happy, and that she didn't deserve joy. But she prayed none the less for God to let her die, and that would make her happy. And so she prayed and prayed, with her stomach wrenching in pain, only saying two things until she fell asleep: "Protect my family," she cried to God. "Let me die."

The next day came and Mary was filled with conflicting emotions once again. She felt ashamed for her action the night before, but she also felt some regret for not finishing what she had started. Mary was sad and tired and angry and anxious about her upcoming therapy. She took a shower hoping to piece together some of her feelings, but found nothing good in the warm water. After a bit of disappointment she decided to get dressed. She thought about not going to the therapy, but then her guilt over burdening her family came back into her mind, and pushed her to finished dressing and then simply deal with the situation as it came. She could almost find strength in her anger, but as many times as it might bring her strength throughout the day, it would always be short lived.

Mary's mother drove her to the doctor's office on that Wednesday morning. It was just before eleven when they arrived at the office. Once again there was not a secretary, and just as before the open door welcomed them. The doctor was sitting at his desk looking at his computer screen, but he heard them come in and smiled.

"I'm surprised to see you ready, most of the other doctors in town take forever," Mary's mother started.

"Well, I like to leave a half hour after each session before the next starts, just in case something big comes up and we need to talk longer, or to get myself prepared. It seems to work out well. I never charge for the time, and sometimes people will open up just so that they can get some free therapy, and that is all that matters to me," he said with a smile.

Mary's mother smiled back, at first out of politeness, but then out of the realization that this man was serious. This man seemed to want to help people, not just finish projects. But she quickly excused herself and Mary sat down and Doctor Ross sat directly across from her in another chair near his desk.

"How are you doing today, Mary," he asked. After he asked his question the two sat silent for fifteen seconds, but the doctor was patient, awaiting her response. What was more surprising was his body. It did not move, nor did he blink as he waited diligently.

"I'm sad."

"Are you tired also?"

"I'm always tired," she complained.

"That's understandable. I'm sorry to hear about your loss. I can't even imagine the tremendous hole it must leave in your heart."

Mary looked up at him. She didn't expect him to say that. Mary thought he would be quick to label her something, and then send her away.

"Yes, it did," she returned.

"How long has it been, since the incident occurred?"

"What day is it?" she asked.

"November the fifth."

"Then it has been one month and twelve days," she responded.

"Then the loss is still fresh. I want you to know that it is perfectly normal to feel sadness after such a passing. There is nothing wrong with still feeling sad, and you may still feel sad a year from now. I want you to know that it is important to feel sad, and that you are not wrong in feeling so."

"Then why am I here," she asked him.

"You tell me," he responded.

His response startled her again, and almost aggravated her a bit. But she thought about the question for a moment as he looked on, none the less.

"I guess that my parents are worried about me."

"Why would they be worried about you," asked the Doctor.

"Because I spend all day in my room, and I cry all the time, and..." In her silence most could detect that she was trying to hold something back. She pushed her head down. "Because I spend all day in my room, and I cry all the time."

The doctor not being fooled by her quick response questioned her. "Is there any other reason you think they would be worried?"

"No, that is all that they see."

"So there is more trouble than just what they see?"

"I don't know how any of this matters," she started in frustration. "I shouldn't even be here, I'm not crazy, I'm just sad!"

"No one said you are crazy. We can come back to that later. Tell me about your children."

"I don't really want to talk about them, it makes me sad."

"Can you try and tell me something that you remember about them during a really happy time, maybe while they were playing or something," he asked patiently.

"I can't remember any good things. I can't remember any happy times, only sad and frightening times," she said getting frustrated.

"So you can't remember one time when you saw them smile?"

"Well, no, well, I don't know."

"Let's make a deal. You tell me one happy time, just try and think one up, and then we won't talk about it again for a while. How about that?"

"Okay, fine," she said. "There was a time when they were smiling helping me make some brownies and they were licking the bowl and spoon," she said very quickly. "Okay, now can we go on?" She stared up at his eyes with a cold expression.

"You bet," he responded with a smile. She couldn't understand why he smiled all the time. Had he not stopped smiling since she came into the office? "Can you tell me anything about your late husband?"

"Ugh, why are you doing this to me?"

"Bringing up the past?"

"Yes! Whenever I think about them, I begin to feel sad."

"Okay, same deal with your husband. I want you to think of one good time when he was alive. You only have to find one."

She thought about it for a moment. "When Michelle was first born, he was so happy. He was standing near the bassinet that he built with the biggest smile on his face as he placed her in for the first time."

"Sounds like a good memory."

"It was," but at the same moment that Mary said it, her faced moved from a smile to a frown again. "Can we move on to a different subject?" she asked.

"In just a moment, but first, I want you to tell me exactly what thoughts came into your mind from the moment of the good memory and any thoughts after that, until you felt sad and wanted to move on. No thought is unimportant, so anything that you remember will be helpful."

"What?"

"Just a moment ago, what did you think?"

"I told you that I saw him with a smile by the bassinet and then I thought..." her faced moved to a frown again.

"There! That! What was that thought right there?" he asked.

"I saw him dead, and it made me sad again."

"Did you just see him dead, or were there any more thoughts?"

"What do you mean," Mary asked intrigued, but confused.

"Did you think of him getting hurt or dying before you saw him dead, or did he just appear in your mind lying still?"

"I don't remember," she replied confused.

"That is okay. What I want you to try and do is every time that you feel sad or down because of your loss, I want you to think of what thoughts you made just prior to the hurt feelings."

"O-Okay."

"Many times a person will see something bad happening to them, like if they were on top of a building and they were afraid of the height. They don't just think about the height, but they imagine themselves slipping and falling, and trying to grab hold of something, and then eventually falling. I want you to think of what thoughts make you sad, and when you do feel sad try and think about what thoughts you had just prior to the sadness."

"Okay, I think I can do that."

Doctor Ross stood up and went over to his desk and got out a small-spiraled notebook and a pen.

"I have these made by an office company," he said. "It has pages with dates and times all in columns made out. Now you don't have to do this every time that you have a bad feeling, but as often as you can, and to your convenience. Use this, and write down what time and day your tough thoughts occurred and what you remember thinking just prior to it, and we will be able to start working." She took it, but didn't think much of it. She looked at the clock on the wall and realized that there were only about twenty minutes left, and her brain felt tired. He was working it a lot since she was there. She had so much information to process, and she could still feel her uneasiness about the entire situation.

The next half-hour or so in the conversation went by without difficult questions for Mary. Doctor Ross was allowing her to just talk about whatever came into her mind, and give him some general information about her life. Mary was almost beginning to like the session, but the doctor could not let her go without some tough questions.

"How do you feel about living with your parents again?" asked Doctor Ross.

"Oh, I was hoping you wouldn't ask me that," she replied. "I like to be independent and I like to be in control of my life. While I'm there, I feel like I'm using them, and not living up to my potential."

"Using them?"

"Yes, I mean that. I don't pay rent, they care for me, and they are paying for this session, among other things."

"You have had a tough string of luck."

"Sure, but I don't want to be cumbersome. I like working my way to my goals."

"That is good that you want to work for what you have. But do you think that you are a burden on them?"

"Well of course I am. I'm staying there without paying for anything and they are taking care of everything, and I'm about crazy without my children, and I hardly get out of bed. They must be going as crazy as I must be! And haven't we just gone over this?"

"You're not crazy. Does this ever make you feel sad? You thinking that you are a burden, I mean?"

"Yes…sometimes. I don't know. Yes, late at night most of the time."

"Times when they can not see or hear you?"

Mary remembered that she had said that earlier in the session. This guy had a good memory. She might have to watch herself, or he could trick her. "Is he trying to trick me?" she thought to herself.

"Yes, late at night when they can't see or hear me, I feel guilty like I'm taking advantage of them, and it makes me feel bad. There I said it!"

"Were your children ever a burden to you?" he asked.

"No! Of course not! They were my children! I was their mother, and I would do anything to help them, no matter what, and they would never be a burden to me!" The question nearly angered Mary. Who was this man to ask her if her children were a burden to her? She loved them dearly. She loved them more than air.

"If your children could *never* be a burden on you, why are you a burden on your parents?"

"It is different. I'm grown, and I'm not a child."

"Say your children had grown, and came into a tough spot in their lives and needed to fall back on you for some time to get back on their feet. Would you have denied them?"

"No! And I know where you are going with this."

"Okay, then, so why again are you a burden to your parents, when you just said that your children could *never* be a burden to you?"

Mary began to get angry. Was this man not listening? She was an adult. She should be strong no matter what. She shouldn't need any help, she was tough and she had made her decision to live on her own long ago. "Because I'm tough. I should be able to take care of myself."

"And if your parents were ill, and you needed to watch over them and take care of them, would you want them to feel like they were a burden on you?"

"No. I would take care of them, and they wouldn't need to worry."

"So they wouldn't have to be as tough as you, because you would be there?"

"That is right, I could be tough for them."

"And your children would never have to be as tough as you, because you would be there?

"No, they would have never needed to be tough if I am there."

"So why are you the only person in your family that isn't allowed to be needy?"

Mary began to get angry. Who was this guy, and what was he trying to do? He was trying to trick her, he must be, why else would he be asking such weird questions! He was a bad man! She got up and kicked her chair over and was about to walk out the door, and was only a step away from the door when he called out.

"Don't forget your notebook," he said smiling reaching it out to her. He stood up and walked over to her with it in his hand. "Just try to do this whenever you can. And try to remember, just try that your parents want you in their lives as much as you want your children. They want to help you, and you don't always have to be the pillar of strength."

With that, Mary left. She was unhappy with the man, but she took her notebook with her nonetheless. She felt that maybe he was right, but what did he know? She stormed out of the waiting area, with her father quite startled that she moved so fast out of the place. He jumped up and looked at the smiling Doctor as he looked out of the doorway. He was there to pick up Mary, and he could see that his daughter was upset. Was this what he was paying one hundred dollars an hour for?

"You ended early?"

"Well, yes. She felt that it was time, but we did a lot of work today. She will probably be angry at me for a few days," started the doctor. Mary's father got a strange look on his face, like he was dumbfounded at what happened. "But that will pass. I hope that she will be back next week."

"I'm sure, Doc," said Mary's father. "I haven't seen her move that fast since she got here, one way or the other, you did her some good!" Mary's father said the words but he wasn't entirely sure that they were true. Maybe he did some good, but what is the point if it makes her cry?

The two shook hands and smiled at each other and Mary just sat in the car contemplating everything that had happened, trying to make sense to it all in her mind. Was he right? No! How could he be right? He was the crazy one? "What am I going to do with this damn notebook?" She thought for the entire trip back home, but her anger subsided quicker than she thought.

He didn't know what he was talking about, because he was just a quack. "No reason to fuss over a quack."

Chapter 7

Mary spent the rest of the evening thinking about what the doctor had told her about being just as important to her parents as her children were to her. How could that be? She was a failure and her children were nothing more than angels on earth. Mary thought that she didn't amount to much and that she had accomplished nothing in life, and although her children hadn't accomplished many things, she should be expected to do better. She was older. But her children did accomplish one very powerful thing. They made her happy, totally and completely. She never thought that she needed anyone in her life until they came along. Mary imagined her children playing in the park, smiling, and enjoying the warm summer day. She saw the images in her mind, them swinging in the park with the sun shinning on their faces, and their teeth being shown in their smiles. Michelle helping Emily with Mary directly behind them to watch them and take care of the little one. They got along so well, better than most siblings ever could. They were the lights of Mary's life. But that was all gone. The only part of her once perfect life that remained intact was that of her own flesh. She no longer had a mind or heart as she had before, but now a soulless empty shell of a person haunted day and night by the remnants of a good life.

Mary finished her thought of her children happy, and then she imagined the truck hitting the side of the car with Michelle on the left side, the first to receive the impact, killing her nearly instantly, and then Emily in pain as she was rushed to the hospital. And the thought quickly led to reminding Mary of Emily's twitching body as the doctors tried to revive her. Mary saw the crash again in her mind, watching as the metal from both vehicles twisted and forced the glass to fly into her children's faces, and the crushing power of the impact destroying the life that she loved so much. Mary suddenly realized that she was crying again, and very sad. Was this what the doctor was talking about? Why should she waste her time feeling sad, and dealing with the pain, if she had to remember the thoughts, then it would just bring back pain? What was he trying to accomplish? She found herself sitting at the end of her bed after the long time of pacing with tears making their way slowly down her cheeks, and she looked over at the notebook that Doctor Ross had given her.

She stood up quickly, and with tunnel vision seeing only the notebook, and nearly ran to the book, picked it up and threw it across the room and into the wall. With the crash that it made slamming up against the wall, almost as if her body was hit with the same shock, she fell to the ground remembering good times and tough times, not only with her children, but also with her late husband. Why did the doctor make her think about her thoughts? Why was he torturing her like this? What did he want from her? And why would she have to constantly remind herself with that damned notebook?

The next morning came and she found herself in her bed. She felt rested, but she wasn't quite sure how she got there. The last thing that she remembered was falling asleep crying on the floor, but that was at only five o'clock yesterday. Did she sleep all night? Her father must have put her into bed, since she was wearing the same clothes. She could see the sun coming in through her window although the cold weather was still plaguing her. She would receive no accommodation from the winter as it would only get worse and worse, since the winter months ran so late there. The cold mornings of November were angering her, but before she could get the energy to be angry on that morning, she felt tired again. "How can I do that?" she asked herself. "How can I wake up and feel so alive and awake, and then with just a few thoughts about my family or the cold weather be tired all over again?"

Although she didn't want to get out of bed, she felt that she should do it for her family. They were paying for her to go to that quack of a doctor, but she shouldn't waste their money, and at the very least make it seem as though she was feeling better, although she couldn't see it herself. She took her usual morning shower, and was quite indifferent to the warmth. Although it brought refuge from the cold air that found its way through the glass, she didn't really care. She didn't need comfort. She did not deserve it. She had killed her family and now she was wasting her life away. Mary could not make sense of why she was still around. She dressed herself and talked quietly and somberly to God.

"Why am I still here? What purpose can I still have in life? I have no family to care for. I have nothing to watch over and keep out of harms way. My whole life I've been the person that has been there for others, and tried to help them, and as soon as my kids were born, they became my mission, but I failed miserably at that. Why did you take them away from me?" she asked finding her way to her room and sitting on her bed again. "Was I horrible at some point in time? Did I disappoint you? I tried to be a good person, but why did all of this happen to me?" Mary stayed very calm while talking to God. Lately she didn't want to yell or argue to the Big Guy. She just wanted to talk with Him, and hope that something would come out of it. "I know that you work in mysterious ways, but isn't this enough? Let me leave this place. I'm tired, and I'm lonely, and I have no hope. Why God, why? Please let me die."

Mary shook off her thoughts and finished getting dressed. She wanted to do something with her life for the first time since her children passed. She wanted to prove to her parents that they weren't wasting their money. Although she was a burden to them and spending their money and time, she would prove to them that she was a child to be loved and that she was worth something. She wanted to prove her worth, and today she would do something great to prove that. But on the revelation that she couldn't do anything great, she became depressed again. She was on her way down the stairs when she realized that she just couldn't get up and do something great, so why even try? Mary nearly convinced herself to go back up to her room when her father walked by the stairs and saw her. His warmth and pride to see her out of her room inspired her to continue on.

He smiled, looking at her in awe as she made her way to the breakfast table. Her mother had made enough for three, just like every morning, but it seemed that her allotment of food would be eaten for the first time in months. Mary looked at her dumbfounded parents as she took a seat. She didn't want to deal with a lot of questions, so she just ended their speculation.

"Mom; Daddy. I just wanted to try, since you are working so hard for me, I just wanted to show you that I want to do good with my life, and that I'm not a waste of your money."

Her father realized that she didn't want to talk about it, but before the moment ended he put in his two cents with a stern and serious demeanor, "You are never a waste of our money or our time. We love you, no matter what." And with that he went back to his breakfast with a great smile on his face.

Mary looked intently on his smile. She watched his face wrinkle as the muscles worked to produce a smile. The showing of teeth is more, to people, than just a movement of the body. It produces chemicals that make you feel happy, and those same chemicals trigger it. It was a strange thing to Mary though. She hadn't smiled for the longest time and she just didn't know why. She was never happy-that was part of it. She hadn't laughed or made any jovial sounds whatsoever for as long as her children left her. The three seconds or so of his smiling seemed to last an eternity to her, and she was paralyzed at the thought of her own smile. She hadn't seen it in so long and she didn't even want to force a fake one. But Mary discontinued her thinking and enjoyed her breakfast for the first time in the last month.

The next five days went by more quickly than the previous, partly because she was moving around more now. Instead of just lying in bed crying, or sleeping for no reason, she found herself arguing, not only with God, as before, but with her own mind more. Mary also found herself pacing endlessly like she was put on a pendulum on a clock, she would just go back and forth, back and forth, while the sun made its way from one side of the sky to the other. She kept looking at the dumb notebook that the doctor gave her as well. She had worked in it seven times in the five days. She didn't really understand why she was doing it. The doctor had told her that she wasn't pressured or anything. But she was always one to do her homework, even though she hated it. Mary recalled times when she was younger, forcing herself to be better, and stronger, and as long as she could remember, she wanted to be in control of her own life; make her own decisions. Mary remembered research assignments taking hours on end, but she would not finish until they were nearly perfect or as perfect as she could hope to get them. She remembered other projects with other children, and she would do so much work, not simply because they didn't want to work hard, but she liked to do things herself, and she didn't like to be dependent on her fellow students for her grade. The thought described her feelings that she held now and for the last few years of her life. No matter the difficult situation, Mary would find a way to cover for herself. This thought made her somber again. She ran through her mind the work and despair she was putting her parents through and she lost herself again and fell back into tears. It was no longer just her children that she would cry about, but everything.

She didn't even know why she was still home. Her children haunted her, yes, but could she go on, could she be stronger? Was she burdening her parents for no reason? Was she a waste? Mary couldn't think, so she stopped trying. She cried for a while, not knowing for sure why, but thinking that it couldn't hurt to cry, but she soon regained her composure to see the notebook staring at her. How did it get on the lamp? "Did I put it there?" She knew that her breakdown had some thoughts before it, that might have "caused" her tears. Should she write them down? Would this matter to the doctor? They weren't thoughts of her family, but of her own life. Should she? She stood up and moved closer to the lamp. She eyeballed the notebook and finally picked it up.

She opened it to an empty page and wrote in the time and the day. She described her thoughts of waste for her parents and her discouragement from thinking. She described how she couldn't even think of why she was crying or what was happening in her life, or how she couldn't make sense of what was going on in her mind. Mary kept writing of how she felt as though she was pulled in different directions at once. The writing was scribbled and blotchy, but there was four times as much writing as any of the other entries. She seemed to let go, and at the end her hand hurt and she was tired of herself. "You aren't worth anything," she told herself. "Why are you having to go through this? Why are you worthless?" she screamed in her mind. She threw the notebook again and sat down. The rest of the day went without much interference, and with no other work in the notebook. She was tired.

Chapter 8

The next day came, and Mary woke up to see the sunlight again; but just as before the cold air found its way into her room. "Damn cold air haunting my existence. Why can't it just be seventy degrees day in and day out?" She got up, none the less, and made her way to the shower. She was trying to take a shower every morning again. She had practically given it up for a while, but in order to feel as though she was pleasing her parents, she would try and shower every day. But it wasn't getting any easier as the days went by. Mary got into the shower and thought of how she must have been pleasing her parents, but before the thought ended she thought of all of the other hassles that she had given them. Mary couldn't think of how taking a shower could even place a dent in the structure of inconveniences that she had already laid down. Mary was troubled by this thought, and felt saddened again. It seemed to work like that all the time. She would think about not being up to par or her children and she would go from a mood that was not bad into one that was. She was hardly ever in a good mood, and still did not smile, but how did her indifferent mood change so quickly?

Mary dressed herself in warm clothes. She thought about wearing sweatpants, but the thought that she was losing her figure made her angry and depressed, so she decided to squeeze into some tight jeans. She bundled up and her father warmed up the car for their trip to Doctor Ross. The trip there was quiet just as normal, but Mary's father seemed pleased that she was going, and unlike what the doctor had thought, she came willingly and didn't make a fuss that day or any of the prior days. Mary wasn't one to fight with her family, but the doctor did not know that yet. Mary stepped out of the car when it came to a stop and she looked up at the steps traveling to the office. She looked at her watch and realized that she was only five minutes early. She liked to be more early than that, but she shrugged off the idea knowing that there would be plenty of time to punish herself later. She walked up the stairs and into the office doorway. She went down the hall and found that the doctor's door was open just as normal, and Mary's father let her go from there, and Mary walked into the office, knocking on the door.

"Oh, Hello, Mary! Come on in, and take a seat, please," with a motion of his hand.

She did as he wished and found her seat. Moments later he sat down in his chair across from her, and with the same smile that he had constantly, he looked her in the eyes. He noticed that she brought the notebook with her and smiled.

"How are you today?" he asked.

"Okay, I guess."

"Okay! Well that is great!"

She was confused. Why was he so happy that she was okay? "Why are you so thrilled that I'm okay," she replied out loud for him?

"Well because the first time that we met you said that you were sad. And then on our first session, I asked you how you were doing on that day and you said that you were sad, but today you said that you were okay. That is awesome!" he said enthusiastically, but she didn't seem to share his joy, and he knew it.

Doctor Ross calmed his face and looked right into her eyes once again. "I know that you think that I'm crazy, and you probably think that I'm a quack, and you probably think that I am a waste of time and money."

She didn't give him a response to what he was saying; she just stared right back at him. "And you could be right," he continued. "I could be a quack, I could be crazy myself, and I probably do get too excited too easily, but I *am* excited to see a change in your demeanor, even slightly. And as I said before, you should feel sad for the loss of your children, but I'm not sure if that is the reason you are here, and I'm betting you don't know exactly what the reason is either."

Once again she didn't have a response for him, but who could have a response? What was a person to say to something like that? She didn't know why she was there, she just knew that it was tough to get out of bed and that her parents wanted to make it easier on her some how and she didn't want to let her parents down, so here she was. He looked at her still.

"Did you have the time to do any work in your notebook; I see you brought it with you?"

"Yes, a little," she responded. "He sure does talk a lot," she thought to herself.

"That is good," he said, this time controlling his pleasure. "How many entries did you make?"

"Eight."

"Eight! That is great. Eight is more than most people do on their first week. Are there any entries that stand out in your mind, maybe one or two that you could almost feel what this exercise was for?"

"I-I don't know."

"Do you mind if I look at it?" She didn't say anything, but handed him the notebook. He opened it and looked at the four pages that had writing in them. He read through them quickly, but flipped to the last page to see the last entry.

"Wow. This one is many times longer then any of the others. This last one, I mean."

"And?" she questioned uninterested.

"Well, lets go over this one for just a minute," he said. He read over it again for just a second. "You were confused at this time?"

"Yes," she responded.

"So you remember making this entry?"

"Well, sure, it was yesterday, and I'm not that crazy yet."

"What were you confused about?"

"I don't know. I guess I was worried about displeasing my parents and wanting to be strong, but then I guess I was fighting with myself about it."

"Go on," Doctor Ross urged.

"Well, I know that for some reason that we haven't figured out yet, I'm having a tough time with everything. And part of me wants to just be a burden and get away from life for a bit, and just feel bad. All the while another part of me is pushing to be strong and to fend for myself, and making me feel sorry for that time that I'm spending feeling sad."

"I think I understand," said the doctor.

"So I don't know. I was just confused." The doctor nodded his head for a second.

"Well, lets go over this again. Remember last week, how talking about this made you angry. But I want you to know that it is okay to be angry and even though it is not always good for you to let out your aggressions we are going to let those slide for now. So if you feel like kicking my chair again, that is fine, we can even paint on a little bull's eye on it, just in case."

The remark made Mary smile and laugh just a bit, and at the very moment, she covered her mouth with her hand, and her eyes seemed as stunned as they could be. She hadn't smiled since her children left, and she didn't even think about it. She had just smiled. Her thought that this was a strange doctor was suddenly amplified. She was blank. She couldn't think. Her mind was filling with thoughts, she felt sad, but she couldn't figure out why she had laughed and smiled.

"What is wrong?" he asked her.

"I-I-I don't know."

"What do you mean?"

"Well I know what is wrong," she started again. "I smiled."

"Is that a bad thing?"

"I haven't smiled since before the accident. I just was not in the mood to smile, and it has been so long, and the sensation was strange to me."

"That is cause for celebration then, a simple smile."

"I'm almost scared," she said putting her hands to her mouth again.

"Why?"

"I don't know."

"Have you ever told yourself that you don't deserve happiness?"

She looked at him with a blank look on her face again. It was almost as if he was in her brain. How did he know that? Why did he ask her that? Should she lie, if she said yes, then she would be crazy, he would surely say she was crazy then?

But she did not have a chance to answer before he interjected again. "It is okay if you have. We all have at some point, really; well anyone that has been really depressed before. It is something that we say to ourselves. You know there was a time when I was very depressed, when I was younger, and I said that to myself a lot. Would you like to know why people who are down say that to themselves?"

She nodded. Mary was still in awe of the situation and she didn't like thinking that she might be crazy, and these probing questions made her doubt her own mind.

"We say that because when we are depressed we don't think that we are worth anything. And if we are not worth anything, then we feel that someone else deserves the happiness. We think that, and then we think that we can't do anything right, and of course we hardly ever do something fantastic when we are depressed, because we are too depressed at the time. It is a downward spiral. I have felt it before."

"Oh, that is just great. My shrink is just as crazy as I am." Again in her mind, "He sure does talk a lot. Aren't we here to talk about me!"

"It feels good to smile, doesn't it?" he asked.

She looked at him, yes, but her mind went to a negative place again, and her disposition moved back to a somber one, and her face quickly portrayed her feelings of uselessness.

"What was that thought, just then?" inquired the doctor.

"I don't know. I saw myself happy and smiling and it just seemed so far away, like a walk that I couldn't make, so I guess that I just gave up."

Doctor Ross leaned forward. He had not taken his eyes off of her for the entire session so far. He was so tentative, and it made Mary feel eerie. "That road is very long. It is very hard to travel it alone, but that is what I'm here for. I'm not saying that you will not be sad, or that you won't ever get depressed once you finish that walk, but you will feel better. We can get you there. You could do it yourself, but as you just felt, it is a long and hard road. I can't do it for you either. But, we can if we help each other. It will still be hard and long, but you will have someone to help you along the way, but I can't help you unless you can believe that you can make it."

"I don't know if I can believe that," she responded.

"Then believe, that next week we can make you feel just a little better. Not a lot, not a bunch, not a hard road, but just a little, that is all that you have to believe right now. Can you believe that much?"

"I guess, I don't know."

"I'll tell you this. You have eight entries in your notebook, which is indeed a good accomplishment. If you can make it ten within the next week, or seven again with longer entries and more thoughts, then that will help you to believe. Baby steps, baby steps."

She simply stared at this strange man. What was he trying to do? The rest of the session went by quickly, and the doctor didn't pry very much, and she seemed happy with that. Mary didn't like it when he pried into feelings that she knew made her feel bad. How would that help anything to bring up poor thoughts that only made her feel bad? She finished the entire session and walked out to her father. On her way out, he yelled, "Remember the notebook," and that was all.

Her dad asked her what he meant by that and she showed him the notebook, but didn't let him read what was inside. She explained it a little bit, but didn't give him any information that might make him worry, or give him the opportunity to pry. She wanted to keep all of this to herself for that time, and later if the time was right reveal her thoughts.

Mary still didn't know what to do though. She still believed that she didn't deserve happiness and ease. She believed that she needed to earn back the respect that she had before, and earn her happiness as well, but that was a road just as long as the one bringing her back to a happy time. She was in a melancholy mood leaving the office. She wanted to feel better and she wanted to work and get back her life, but it seemed like an unattainable and torturous trial. Could she trust him to help her through this? What would happen if she didn't do more with her notebook? Would he stop letting her come? Would he do that? Could he? "Well if anyone would deserve it, it would be me," she thought to herself. "I'm about as useless as it gets."

The rest of Mary's day went by slowly as the thought about this "getting better." She didn't even know if she really wanted to be better, she liked feeling heavy hearted. She needed to be sad from her loss. She wanted to cry for her children and for her lost husband and for her destroyed life. The doctor said it was okay, so why was she going to see him? That was the same question that he had asked her. Why would he ask that question? "I'm tired." Her mind was weary and she decided to go to sleep. And that night, just like most other nights, she would cry a bit when thinking of her children, but it was okay, the doctor said so. She would release her tears and her energy would flow out with the droplets and slowly her eyes would become as heavy as her heart and she would fight it no longer, and she would sleep.

The next morning came and Mary forced herself to get up and take a shower, but the warm water felt chilled as she kept thinking that she was still a burden on her parents and that they would not want her to be there anymore. Mary, for some time, stared blankly into the wall and peered deep into the tiles. It seemed as though her mind was put on cruise control as she measured each crevice from tile to tile with her eyes. But her mind did find its way back and she felt depressed and was angry with herself. These episodes happened once or twice a day; it seemed. She would be angry with herself, to the point of even slapping herself, and then forcing her body to regain its composure. She felt that this was one of those times that the doctor was talking about, and with a gathered will, she decided to write in her notebook. She forced her hand to write it out very completely, so that the doctor would be pleased with her efforts. She wanted to please him, just as she did her family. She almost felt as though she owed him her hard work. And while writing about her thoughts and remembering them, almost to the point of anger again, she remembered also, her childhood. She remembered the will power that it took to force her mind and body to work hard and do the work necessary to do well. She hadn't felt that in a scholastic way in quite a while. The feeling gave her strength.

The rest of that Thursday went by without any other breakdowns, but she still didn't feel like leaving her room. Her self-defeating thoughts hid in her mind, and although they were not present, their power lingered still, and Mary knew that they could come back at any moment. Her life looked as though someone had medicated her and she hadn't come down from it yet. She would just stare at the walls and think of days gone by and joys that she had lost. For the longest time Mary would be off in a distance, completely unaware of the happenings around her. She was tired of the world being happy and leaving her behind, but she didn't have the energy to get up and do anything about it. Even if she had the energy, the tasks seemed so hard and it just didn't matter. It couldn't bring back her family; she was lost one way or the other.

Mary did find a way to take a break in her trance to eat lunch and dinner, which gave her mother great pleasure. Just before she went to sleep, she thought about the two smiles and laughs that she had in Doctor Ross' office, but those moments of levity seemed so far away already. She couldn't bring herself to smile now though. She thought about the motions of a smile and decided that before she would go to sleep, she would force a smile. Fake or not, it did not matter, she would make a smile again. She fought with herself, and yelled at herself. "If you want to get better then we have to fight for it. Now let's fight for it!" she told herself. She got up from her bed and walked to her vanity that held a mirror. She sat down in the little chair there and looked at her mouth. She felt the muscles move, but she could not even force a smile. "Force it!" she screamed to herself. "You can do this, you can be strong," but still no effect. "Fine, I give up. No! You can't give up, this is important. But it can't be done. It can! Force it. You are stronger than this; you are tough. I'm worthless. Maybe so, but even a worthless person can smile, so get your ass into gear!"

She moved her muscles and her face produced a disfigured strange smile, but she kept yelling at herself. "Do it! We don't go to sleep until this happens. Make it happen, it is your life!" She moved her muscles again and saw a true to form smile make its shape. Joy boundless streamed through her. "I did it. I did it. Oh my God." She smiled for a moment longer and it became a real smile. She jumped up and began to write it down in her notebook. She had forced a smile, but while writing she lost her glee and remembered hard times, but her will forced her to write that into her book as well. It took her almost ten minutes to write down all of her feelings including her transition from gloom to happiness back to gloom. She closed the book, when she finished, and walked to her bed confused and tired. She quickly fell asleep after putting her thoughts away.

When Mary awoke the next morning it was out of a dream. She seemed to feel asleep and awake at the same time, as most people do after dreams, but she shook it off only to see her room as it had always been. The lavender color seemed to scream at her of boredom. She just looked around her room and as normal she looked out one of her windows to see her elm and the cold air seeped into her room as normal. She continued her view of her room and saw that not much of it had changed since her childhood. She remembered times when she was in high school wondering if a boy would call her to go out on the weekend, and she would stare at her tree, even then, and hopes for the phone to call. She realized that it was Friday. She thought for an instant that maybe she would go out that night. "Ha, whatever. I don't even want to leave my room."

Her friend Pam, who only sustained minor injury during the crash, would call every now and then, but Mary's mother had told her the same thing time after time: "She is too tired." Mary knew that some truth found its way into what she said, but it wasn't even close to the whole truth. "I guess that Mom just doesn't want other people to think that I am crazy or that I might be a failure. I am a failure though." Mary got out of bed in an indifferent mood and once again forced herself to the shower.

After finishing her shower, Mary looked at herself in the mirror. As she stood there naked before the tall mirror. She was still just as thin as she was in high school, and she had hardly gained any weight since her children's passing, in fact with her loss of appetite, she had probably dropped a considerable amount of weight. She had always been thin, though she worked out a lot, and ran a lot when she had her children to get rid of the baby fat. She looked at her breasts to see that they were never very big, but she didn't mind since her waist was still thin. Not many women that had two children had the figure that she had, but even though she was in good shape and looked good, she could not see happiness in the looking glass. She felt that she was incomplete. She saw herself as useless and worthless. It was Friday and she would not go out that night, nor did she yearn to do so. Her days of going out were over, and she never even minded. She loved being at home with her husband and children. She never really liked dating, she loved the idea of just relaxing, seeing her husband, knowing that he would never cheat on her or leave her. But he did leave. Doctors found cancer in him and he was taken away, along with all of her money and life. And then she tried so hard to bring her life back together and her children became her reason for living and then they were taken too! And now here she was standing in front of the mirror with the body that God gave her and with the years he had given her; could think of no accomplishment she could give to her name. She just gazed into the mirror wishing for the past. She felt that her life was hopeless, and it did not seem to make her feel better when she thought of her therapy. "That is even worse. I have to have help to get back to where I was. I got there on my own, so what happened?" She stood in front of the mirror and broke down into tears. The chill of the air as she cooled down and became cold and goose bumps rose up from her skin. She cried, shivered, and sat on the bathroom floor, completely destroyed again. It took her twenty minutes to regain her composure and to reassure herself that clothes were an important part of life. She got back up, looked at herself in the mirror as she dressed herself still unhappy with her life and discouraged. Mary did not believe that she could get better, but the doctor said that she didn't have to. She only had to do a little more work in her notebook, so that she would do. She could not see happiness, but she would not allow that doctor to get the best of her. She would show him! She wrote and wrote during her morning. "I will show him what I am made of."

And so she wrote, and she took advantage of every major break down that she had for that week before she was to go back to the doctor's office. She made eight entries on the dawn of her day of recognizing, as it would seem. The entries were longer and better; he had to be happy with that. She wasn't a writer, so what more could he want. She unloaded her thoughts and her feelings into that book, from her feelings of loss to her wishes to die to her parents and how they made her feel. There was even one entry about how she didn't believe that she could do adequate work with the notebook and he wouldn't want to see her anymore. The writing was a burden and a release at the same time. She didn't want to feel like she was a nobody, but the more that she thought about not being a nobody and not being useless, she seemed to feel it more and more. How could that be? How could wanting to be something more or better find a way to make her feel worse about everything in her life?

She stood outside with the bitter cold air on her face as she waited for her Dad to get ready to leave. She didn't want to be inside, she felt that the air did her justice for all of her wrong actions in life. Mary thought about how the cold air could be killing the cells of her skin one by one from the top of her skin layers right down to the bottom, and how the destruction made justice for all of her sins. She was doing more thinking with God and she felt that she was guilty of so much, and all that had happened to her must be her punishment for her destructive lifestyle. That didn't seem to make sense, but every time that Mary thought that she did not deserve the Hell, she over exaggerated some small transgressions through her life. How, oh how a small offense to her parents killed her now, but "I deserve it," she thought to herself. "I am paying for my crimes right now. The only problem is that I don't deserve to get an end to my sentence. Those whom I cared for were not given mercy. Why should I?"

Her father found his way out and they went to the car. The ride over was just as quiet as it was always. The truth was that Mary hadn't even really talked to her Dad in months. They had a few passing words here and there, but Mary just felt as though she could not have a conversation with him. She was still ashamed that she wasn't out on her own, doing her own life, and preparing for the future. She felt that she was not living up to his expectations and until she found herself in a better situation, she would just go on without many interactions. She still didn't know how to handle her life and that was killing her as much as anything.

She walked into the office room, and the door was open as always. Doctor Ross was sitting at his desk reading as he was the prior two times, but with a slight knock at the door, he arose to see Mary's face.

"Oh, hello Mary. Please have a seat." He got up and moved to his same normal brown chair directly across from her as always. "How are you today?"

Mary had remembered the conversation last time, and she didn't know how to respond. He seemed to make such a big deal about it last time, she didn't want to upset him or give him a false sense of her happiness, which was still very lacking.

"I don't know," she responded.

"Hey, that is all right. I'm not sure how my day is going either," he said with a smile. "Did you have a good week?"

"No. I just stayed inside like I do everyday. It is too cold to do anything anyway."

"Yes, I know. It snowed so much that I was almost unable to get out of my house the other day, but I'm glad to see that the roads are somewhat clear. Did you have any problem today in getting here?"

"No."

"Well that is good. Were you able to do any more work with the thoughts that lead to bad feelings?"

"Yes," she said, handing him the book.

"Do you mind if I read over it?"

"You're the doctor."

He read over them briefly, not wanting to waste too much time.

"Do you know why I have you do this exercise?"

"No," she responded without emotion.

"Well, it allows you to see what thoughts lead up to sad feelings. Like if you were thinking about a happy point in time in your life, you mood would be elevated, but if just after that your thoughts changed to something negative. A negative thought like imagining your children in pain can easily lead to saddened feelings."

"But I thought you said that it was okay for me to feel sad when I think about my children."

"It is, but that is only the beginning."

"I don't know what you mean."

"That is okay. Why is it hard for you to get out of bed in the morning?"

"I don't know," began the now aggravated and confused Mary.

"A lot of times people will not only have thoughts that make them sad, but they will be accompanied by thoughts that express a loss of reason to live, or a negative outlook on life. Do you have any of those feelings?"

"Yes, sometimes."

"Can you live without your children?"

"I haven't decided yet."

"What do you think when you remember that your children left and that you are now more alone then you were."

"I feel like nothing I can do ever matters, like no matter what I do, I can never have my life back. I don't see that light at the end of the tunnel like you do. I can't be happy! I tell you that I will try to do better from last week to this week, and maybe I'll feel better, but I don't want to, and I don't care!" Mary didn't even seem to realize but her voice was greatly raised as her aggravation mounted.

"How do you feel about your late husband?"

"Now I guess that you are just trying to get me going, aren't you? The last boyfriend that I had beat me and ended up in prison, and he was just the end of a long line of losers that I dated in the last two years, hoping to fill that void not only in my heart, but those of my children as well. But they are gone now, and I'm left with even a bigger void! I don't want to be happy again, and I doubt that I will ever meet a man that I would love as much as I loved Gerard."

"You don't want to be happy anymore?"

"No, why? Should I be? I can't imagine myself happy with anyone else. I don't want anyone else to fill that void, I want them!"

"That doesn't mean that you can't be happy."

"How could I be happy with that void in my heart? How can I even live for that matter?"

"You have seemed to do okay with this living part so far."

"My life isn't living. I stay indoors all day long, I don't do anything, I don't have a job, and I live with my parents!" she yelled more.

"And that bothers you?"

"Yes, it does!"

"Why would that bother you if just a few minutes ago you said that you didn't even want to be happy anymore? If you aren't happy, and you don't want to be happy, what does it matter if you live with your parents?"

"Because I shouldn't bring them down with me!"

"Now we are back to the burden issue. Do you still see yourself as a burden to them?" he asked.

"Yes, I don't know. I understand your point, but it is hard for me to think of myself as anything but a burden. I mean really, I have never been good at anything. How can I be anything but a failure."

"Those are strong words, but I don't think that they are true, and I don't think that you believe them either," the doctor responded with calm words.

"What?" she asked.

"Well, you said that have never been good at anything. It sounds like you were a good mother to your children."

"How could I be a good mother if their father died and I put them through a horrible man that scared them, and then I didn't take them to the park myself, so they ended up dying in someone else's car! How could that mean that I was a good parent?" sounded the perturbed Mary.

"Both your late husband's death and the death of your children was not your fault. You had no hand in those," replied Doctor Ross calmly.

"Well I might not have anything to do with my husbands death but I still put my children through those other guys, and I should have been the one taking them to the park, I should have been spending time with them!"

"Let's look at this for a second Mary. Why did you start dating again after you husband died?"

"Because I was lonely and haven't we gone over this?"

"You didn't do it so that you could provide a father figure for your children, or another financial help for them, or maybe even extra time to spend with them?"

"Well of course I wanted that also."

"Then Mary, you didn't put them through a horrible man. You did what you thought might help them. You weren't just dating for you, Hell; you probably were still upset about your husband. You did that for them."

"But that didn't stop the last guy who attacked us."

"Those actions were his decisions, not yours. You can't always know how a person will react to a stressful situation. He did the beating, not you. Did you get your children away from him?" Doctor Ross was still soft spoken, not allowing his energy of the subject get away from his control.

"Yes, we moved because I needed a fresh start and he was going to get out of jail too quickly."

"So you moved to help your children?" he asked.

"Yes."

"Okay, then let's sum this up. You had bad luck that hurt you and your children. You worked as hard as you could to provide for them, you tried to find a good father figure for them, when you had more bad luck there, you moved them and forced yourself to start all over. And even more, you forced yourself to deal with the hurt pride that living with your parents dealt to you. Mary, you did that for your children!"

"And so I moved them here," she yelled. "And then look! They would have been better off if I stayed in St. Paul!"

"Not all situations are under your control," Doctor Ross said.

"Bad luck! I should have been the one to take them to the park and spend time with them."

"What were you doing when your children were hit by that truck?"

"I was working." Mary started to cry just a bit with her face flushed. She kept thinking about all of the bad things that had been happening to her, and she could hardly control her thoughts, but it was of no matter; Ross kept his questions coming.

"You were working so that you could do what?" he pursued.

"So I wouldn't have to live with my parents, so I wouldn't be a burden on them."

"And so, in turn, you could provide for your children?" he asked.

"Well of course, that is a given!" She lost a few more tears.

"And even though you were working, you took a chance for them to get out and get to play with other kids after a tough move, with a person that you knew; that was safe and nice. You wanted your kids to be healthy and happy."

Mary hung her head down and shook it back and forth. "But they died that day!"

"And it was no fault of your own. You did everything in the last two years of you life to protect and provide for them!" He reminded himself to clam down and not become too emotional and began again. "You were a good mother, and you still are as you mourn them."

Mary was in more tears and was almost balling. "Why are you doing this to me?"

"Because this is important, Mary. You have been a good mother, and your children did not die from some fault of yours."

"No, I can't believe that," she said.

"You must. It is the truth. The whole conversation we just had, you told me how much you did for them. You did it all for them."

Mary's head was spinning. She didn't know what was happening. What was the doctor trying to do to her? Why was he making her cry? "I can't believe it," she said again.

"It came from your own lips!" he reacted.

Mary got angry and, with tears pouring down her face, she stood up, slapped Doctor Ross across the face and pushed her chair down, and then ran out of the room. Her father was there that day out in the waiting room, as she came running to him with tears streaming and put herself in his arms.

"I want to go home, Daddy," she said. "I want to go home, Daddy!" she said louder.

"Okay, Darling, okay."

He took her out of the office and didn't look back to see Doctor Ross standing at the doorway watching them leave. She cried all the way home, and didn't respond to any questions from her parents and she just went to her room and cried.

Chapter 9

Just a few hours later the phone rang. Mary thought that it might be the doctor calling to either apologize or at the least explain his actions. Why would he have to apologize? He was only doing his job, right? She battled with the thought in her head, but her first assumption was correct, as it was the doctor calling.

"Hello," answered Mary's father.

"Hello sir, this is Doctor Ross."

"What happened today?" he screamed. "She hasn't answered any of our questions. The first day that she went she left early and was crying, and today it happened again. What is happening?"

"Sir, I can't tell you our conversation. What I can tell you is that in depression, it is very easy for a patient to blame him or herself for the smallest of things and find him or herself useless. With some patients, when they begin to realize that they are not at fault of something that they felt tremendous guilt from, he or she can react in tears or even violence with that epiphany of emotion."

"Does she feel guilty about her children?" he asked.

"I can't talk to you about what transpires in my office, but I just wanted you to know that she is never in harms way while in my office."

"Well, you seem pretty level headed, Doc. And lucky for you, I want her to feel better and if it takes a few hard knocks to get there, then the end justifies the means."

"Thank you for your time sir. I hope to see her next week."

"I'm sure that we can coax her into coming. Have a good night Doctor."

"Thank you, you too. Bye."

"Goodbye."

That night Mary did not get too much sleep. Lately it was easy for her to sleep, it was an outlet, but now her mind was filled. She didn't want to believe the doctor. "How can I not be responsible for what happened?" she asked herself. "I made all of the decisions that led to their demise, and he is sitting there telling me that am not to blame. It seemed so easy to blame herself, how could that be false? "Maybe I'm not to blame," she thought to herself. "No! Then whose fault is it? It must be someone's fault. Why would God do that to me unless I had done something wrong? I have tried so hard to do well. I haven't done any wrong! Maybe I have, I don't know!" she screamed inside her head. She fell over and laid her head on her pillow sobbing. The linen quickly became saturated as her tears continued like a never-ending waterfall. She wanted so badly to believe him, but why couldn't she? Mary kept weeping. Her mind was moving too fast, her emotions were running too high, and she could not keep up with herself. She just wanted to cry and close off those thoughts and feelings.

Hours later she finally picked herself back up; it was eleven o'clock that night. Her parents had brought her some soup while she was crying; she didn't even notice them. She looked at the clock and it surprised her. She had been there crying for six hours.

No wonder she felt dehydrated! Mary walked downstairs and saw the empty living area and kitchen; her parents had gone to bed. She walked into the kitchen and poured herself a glass of water, still trying to figure out her own thoughts. She gulped down the water, and before she could make another thought, she poured another glass and drank it down just as quickly. Her head hurt. She looked through the cabinets and found some aspirin. She thought for a moment that if she just took the entire bottle she wouldn't have to worry for a while. Perhaps it would even kill her, and if not, it would at least put her to sleep for a time. She looked at the label, and noticed the recommendations of two, or at worst four. Mary opened the bottle and decided not to drug herself, but took six anyway. She was tired, her head hurt, and she wanted to sleep, but more importantly, she wanted the pain to go away.

Mary could hardly even sleep though. She tossed and turned until four in the morning, her mind racing about what she and the doctor had spoken about, and the shame she felt for striking him. "I'm no better than that bastard of an ex-boyfriend of mine!" she thought to herself. She was amazed that she could stay awake for so long with the aspirin in her system. Luckily her headache had gone away, and now she could feel sleep coming on, finally. She was tired, and although her headache was gone, her mind was tired. She threw away her thoughts and fell asleep on her still-wet pillow and a melancholy look on her face, fueled with despair and confusion.

Chapter 10

The next day did not bring any clairvoyance on her feelings or on what she should be feeling, but it brought more time of second-guessing, and more tears. Her shower did not bring her better feelings. Mary could not decide whether she was at fault for her children's death or if she was overreacting, but she did feel bad. She felt tired although she slept until almost two in the afternoon. It was not that her body was still tired, but her mind was still tired and she could pull no energy from it.

She went downstairs to get some food. She was hungry and hadn't eaten for the last twenty-four hours. She went down and was greeted by her mother who was vacuuming the carpet. "Hello, Mary. Would you like me to make something for you to eat?"

"No. I'll be fine," said Mary, but her mother held her tongue and knew that forcing her would not help. It was strange though; Mary was confused again as she walked into the kitchen. She hadn't made anything for herself in the last few months, what was happening? She made herself a sandwich, but as she made it she began to feel more and more guilty about hitting her doctor. "Why did I hit him? Was it just because he made me mad? That is no reason to hit a person. Why did I lose control so easily? I don't think I've hit anyone else in my entire life. He probably doesn't want me to come back, but even if he did, I'm not sure if I could face him. He would probably not help me the same; maybe he has already given up on me. I'm sure he has. Why wouldn't he? I'm sure that he can find less crazy patients. Ugh, I'm so worthless." Mary took her abuse to herself and sat down at the dinning room table with her sandwich and a glass of water with her face showing no joy at all.

She ate her sandwich and continued her mope. Mary felt guilty for hitting her doctor and she felt that nothing could ever make up for it. But she did not have much time to think over before her mother came over to her.

"What is wrong, Mary?"

"Which part of me," Mary asked again.

"Ha. That almost sounded like humor, but I'm sure it wasn't," smiled her mother.

"I slapped Doctor Ross during our session," explained Mary, seemingly unashamed in front of her mother masking her feelings well.

"Oh."

"I just got really upset, and he seemed to just keep bringing up more and more upsetting thoughts, and I guess that I just snapped."

"Well, I'm sure that he understands," explained Mary's mother.

"How do you know? He probably doesn't want me to come to his office anymore. I heard the phone ring last night. It was probably him saying that he didn't want me back again."

"Well you are right about him calling, but that isn't what he told your father."

"Really?"

"Yes, actually he was hoping to see you again at the normal time next Wednesday."

"No way, how could he? I feel so bad. He must hate me."

"Well don't worry too much, I'm sure that he won't take it personally."

Mary just shrugged off the conversation and went back to her room to spend time doing absolutely nothing. She left before the doctor could spend any time on her journal of sorts, and she wasn't sure that she would be able to write in it this week, but she was determined to try. That doctor made her so angry though. He had no idea of the mental quagmire that he put her in. She paced her room, angry with him for his words. To him, the deaths of her family were so trivial, but it was harder than he thought! Why did he think that he was in so much control? Mary went through the rest of her day with only one breakdown, but it was as much of diffusion of her thoughts about her guilt as it was her sadness from her losses. Mary still felt guilty for some mistakes through life and felt that she was not worth anything, and during her breakdown she said it many times to herself.

After that, she opened her notebook and wrote down her thoughts and why she thought that the breakdown happened. "I can't remember why he is making me do this," she thought. "I guess he thinks that what I think about causes my sadness. Well I can tell him what causes me to be sad: my children." Mary let the thought pass and went back to her writing. She wrote a lot, but time passed a little more quickly and soon it was late evening. She went downstairs again to see her parents eating dinner and she joined them. Mary's father was stunned and could hardly even speak to see his daughter downstairs eating dinner with them, and although she did not speak while she was there, he was amazed. Mary's father couldn't help to think that the therapy must be doing something for her, one way or the other. He smiled one of his great big smiles as he sat and ate, and, more importantly, watched his daughter eat.

She was an only child and he cared about her more than anyone or anything in his life. He had always wanted more children, but for some reason it just was not to be. His wife and himself had no problems, but they seemed to have bad luck. But his thoughts of his bad luck faded quickly as watching his daughter mesmerized him. Mary noticed his stares, but did nothing to reprimand him. She was simply hungry and could not see what the big deal was about, but she felt conflicting thoughts and emotions on that also. She didn't know how she felt about eating with them. Her father obviously thought that she was getting healthier, but she didn't feel it at all. All she felt was anger and determination to prove to the doctor that she wasn't crazy, and that her children were no trivial matters. She finished her meal and retreated back to her room again and fell asleep quickly, her mind tired from the day.

The next day held no more promise of relief from her misery of thinking, but it did bring more revelations to the mix. Mary woke up and began her day thinking of how it could or could not have been her fault when her children died, but today yielded a different thought than before. Mary envisioned the incident. In her mind she saw, over and over again, a large truck smashing the side of her friend Pam's Toyota and she saw the destructive force in slow motion. She saw the glass break and the side of the door come smashing in and her daughter Michelle being hit with the glass and her head being thrown to the side, and with agony of movement, for a split second, try to move away from the oncoming force. But her daughter would have no such luck as she was pinned down by her own seat belt, but her upper body was thrown up against her little sister, with her arms acting as nightsticks against the smaller child's head. But that was not the end of the destructive onslaught. The momentum of the truck tore the back of the car to pieces, throwing glass and metal through her children and crushing the lifeless body of Michelle onto Emily's and crushing her gentle insides with bone snapping pressure. The thought was in slow motion every time, and for countless times that day Mary thought the incident through. Her children died a thousand horrible deaths that day, all confined to Mary's mind, and it rattled her as her goose bumps from the first vision to the last held strong. She couldn't think of how such a horrible death could have become her children through any fault of her own, but the more and more she saw the destruction, the more and more it wounded her to think that it could have been stopped.

Mary fought herself for hours, not eating lunch, but simply pacing back and forth through the room. The lavender walls seemed to scream at her as she balanced fate and luck, her uselessness, and God's will in her mind. She didn't see how God would have let that happen if she had been a better person, but she felt that the will of a divine being could not be enough, but her misjudgment, as a parent had to play a role. But as she thought it, she saw her children die a horrible death and she could not see how any conscious or unconscious decision of hers could possibly create the deaths of the two things in the world that brought her happiness. Mary was confused and tired, but she kept pacing, weighing the thoughts, back and forth, and then back and forth again. Mary tried to get her mind off of her entrenchment and made her bed, took a shower, cleaned her room, rearranged some of her clothes, but to no avail. Her mind continued its bombardment of itself. Mary could see no end, and as the evening came and she paced, her mother brought her some food. Mary ate it, but her mind was still moving, still thinking.

"How could I be to blame?"

"Well, it must have been me."

"How so?"

"Because I made the decision and God thought I needed the punishment."

"Do you really believe that?"

"I don't know!"

"How else could this have all happened?"

"I don't know!" she screamed inside her head. She fought with herself through dinner and into the late evening, even as her sweat poured down over her body she would not stop her frantic pacing. She fought and fought, and near midnight collapsed into her bed and fell asleep almost instantly. Her body had been in deep thought for two days straight after an afternoon of near Hell. It was time to rest whether she wanted to or not.

After her tiring battle with herself, Mary took the next couple of days to write down all of her thoughts. It took hours it seemed, for her to put down into words all the thoughts that had been invading her mind. Those four days afterwards and then into the fifth day when she was to see the doctor for the fourth time, her mind continued to fight itself, but not nearly to the degree as the first couple of days. She was tired, and maybe she had gotten out all of the energy about the subject and she could now think about it logically. Although the idea seemed like a good one, trying to solve the dilemma of her fault in her children's death turned out to be more of a gauntlet that she had first anticipated.

The following day Mary made it a point to start thinking about her life more logically. She had been strong all of her life in doing, if not the right thing, something on her own. Mary went over in her mind all that day about her feelings, stopping only to eat and shower. Every time that she had brought herself to believe that she was not at fault, her emotions would reject the thought and she would blame herself again, if not for the direct offense, but for some other offense causing it to happen. Mary would blame herself for not spending her time with her children herself, or for trusting them to a person that she hadn't known for years, and someone that her children did not know. If she found a way to talk herself out of blaming herself with those problems, she would force herself to believe that the death of her children was a vengeful act from God to punish her for sins of late. Her guilt didn't seem to go away either, and it even seemed to grow stronger. The more that she though about her guilt, in the eyes of God, the more guilty she felt, for even the most meaningless assailants.

Her guilt would keep her from doing much with her day, but luckily enough she found it relatively easy to fall asleep, just like the night before. Her mind was still tired, and her day of thinking and guilt did not help her to regain energy, but instead, took more away from her. As she went to bed she felt more and more angry with herself for more trivial things.

"Why are you tired?" she would ask herself.

"You haven't done anything all day but walk around, and here you are! You are a worthless piece of crap, and if you weren't, then why wouldn't you be able to solve this problem?" Her angered thoughts to herself forced her into a few tears, but it did not last long as she struck herself in the face.

"Snap out of it! You are stronger than *this*! Or are you?"

"Have you lost your fire? Have you lost your hope? Not like you used it much to start with."

"I did use it; I worked hard, every step of the way."

"And what did you accomplish with it? Huh? Nothing! You ended up with heartache and a lost family, not to mention that you are so weak, here you are with your life wasting it away!"

"I have every right to be depressed!"

"Do you? Why? You weren't doing much with your life to start with."

"That isn't true!"

"Isn't it? If you did so well, why can't you solve this problem? Your children are gone, and you are going to a shrink. You are worthless."

"I'm not! I can get myself out of this."

"Can you?"

"I can!"

"I doubt it."

"Doubt all you want, I'm down, but I'm not out!

"I guess that we will just have to wait and see."

Mary cried, with feelings only of hurt, loneliness, and fatigue. She until her eyes ached and her brow sweat. Then, with no energy to fight on, she fell asleep.

And so came the next day with more logical reasoning. The road was dirty and dusty, but she seemed to think it was still workable as she woke up in the morning. She took her shower and tried not to think of her battles within herself. She dressed and then decided to write in her notebook about what transpired in her mind the night before. She wasn't sure if he could even understand what she was writing, but it wasn't like he spent much time reading over them the last few times, but who was to say he would even skim them this time. Mary still felt guilty over hitting Doctor Ross, and she didn't know how she would react to being in his presence for an hour. Mary swallowed the thought and got back to her writing, determined to do something worth her while that day. Her mind raced as she wrote, trying to articulate exactly what she was feeling. It was hard at first, but it seemed to get easier and easier as page went by after page. Mary was almost tired by the time she finished writing six pages of thinking from the night before.

Mary finished and went back to her thinking, no matter the strain that it pushed on her mind. She argued and paced and stopped only to eat again for that day. As evening came she wrote more in her notebook and feel asleep. Monday and Tuesday went by quicker than the past two days, and those were even faster moving than the two priors were. Mary made it a point to write down more and more of her thoughts and worries and fights with herself. By Wednesday afternoon when she was to go and see her doctor again she had written fifteen pages in her notebook for the week. She thought that in any person's eyes, that was improvement, whether psychologically or not. She dressed herself, worrying about whether or not the doctor would take her kindly. He hadn't sent word that he didn't want her to come back, but he seemed like a man that would keep his word whether he liked it or not. He could make this week her last week. It seemed like she had known him for longer, although this was only her fourth visit. How could that be? He brought out emotions like a waterfall, but she wanted to go again and face him. She was prepared and walked downstairs to see her father ready and waiting.

The drive over there was almost silent as normal, but her father did not let her leave the car without a few words. "I hope that you have a good session. I love you," he spouted with his caring eyes that she always saw.

Mary looked at him for just a moment and gave him a wave. "I love you too Daddy. I think I'm going to stay for the entire hour, no matter what. Okay?"

"Okay, Honey. I'll be around if you need me." He smiled and she was on her way. She moved into the small waiting area and noticed the same painting on the wall that had been there all the times before, and just as normal his door was open, inviting her in as it was the times before. She moved over to the door and walked inside.

As she walked inside Doctor Ross stood up with a smile on his face, as usual. Mary felt a lump in her throat, she didn't feel that she could talk, but forced it out. "I'm sorry," she summoned with a sound gargled and deeper than normal. If she had waited any longer, Mary was worried her stomach would tear itself apart.

"I am sorry as well," he responded. She was puzzled about his apology. "I'm sorry," he continued. "I tried to bring to your attention something that had the possibility of a lot of built up feelings manifesting themselves as anger, and I wasn't prepared for it."

"What do you mean?" she asked.

"I made a mistake in my therapy. I'm sorry to say it, but every now and then we make mistakes with patients and we are not ready for a certain response. I felt it so necessary for you to understand my point, that I lost track of your emotions. For that, I am sorry."

"It is okay, I guess," she responded.

"I'm glad. Although the last session did end on a rough note, it is where we will begin today. I want to work on any angry thoughts that might be dwelling in side of you, so let us just start with the basics."

"Okay."

"Mary, tell me something, unimportant that makes you angry."

"I don't know. Traffic!"

"Excellent, I despise traffic also," he said. "Now tell me something more close to you life that makes you angry."

"I'm angered at myself for having to stay with my parents."

"Why do you stay with your parents if you don't like it?"

"I don't know. I don't have a job."

"Does that make you angry, not having a job?"

"Of course it does!"

"You are smart, and hardworking, I'm sure. Why not go get a job, I'm sure that you could get one?"

"I don't know. I'm tired and hurt. I'm depressed."

"And that stops you from wanting to go out in the morning and find a job, right?"

"That's right!" as her voice raised a bit in response to her growing aggravation with him and his game.

"Does that make you angry?"

"I don't know, a little bit. I'm more angry about this game."

"So you don't think that you are a failure?" he ignored her comment.

"No. Yes, I don't know."

"Do you ever tell yourself that you are a failure?"

Mary didn't want to answer at first, but she complied again. "Yes."

"Why?"

"Because look at me. I'm living with my parents, I have no family and I have no job. How could I not call myself a failure?" Mary felt her emotions gaining more strength.

"You just told me that since you were depressed, not getting a job was justified. And if that is justified, then so must be staying with your parents, or else you would be out on the street."

Mary thought for a moment. Did she say that? What was he trying to do? She was getting more agitated by his ruthless questions. "I don't know," she said.

"You are not a failure. You have had a job before, you were living without your parents, and you have a family."

"I don't have a family!"

"You have your parents," he responded.

"I want my children back, and I want my husband back. They were my family. They were who I wanted in my life." Mary's anger escalated when she thought of them. She was mad at God for taking them away from her, and disappointed in herself for sinning enough for him to take them away.

"You are not at fault for the loss of your children."

"Do we have to do this again?"

"Yes, it is important, but today you can't leave, and if you get angry you have to work through it."

"Okay," she sobbed.

"It's not your fault."

"It is," she cried. Her eyes became red and tears would soon follow with the thoughts of letting down her children.

"You did nothing wrong. You made all the right decisions. You did all that you could and you did it for them!"

"Well if it isn't my fault then whose is it?"

"Maybe it is no one's fault."

"Then, why would it happen? Why would God take them away from me for no reason at all? Why would he hurt me? Does he like to see me in agony?" More tears left her eyes.

"I'm sure that God did not want to put you in pain just to watch you in agony."

"Then why would he do it?" she yelled.

"I don't know."

"You don't know," she yelled again. "You are the doctor! Aren't you supposed to have the answers?"

"I wish that I had all the answers, but some things don't have answers. Just like this."

"It must be my fault," she said again.

"It is not your fault. God does not want to hurt you for his own pleasure. It is not your fault, and it is not some sin from long ago that he wants vengeance for."

Mary could hardly slow her tears down. "Why are you doing this to me?"

"You are a good mother."

"No!" Mary cried more, trying to fight off her own thoughts.

"You are a good mother."

"No," she said again in a whimper.

"You are a good mother, and you are not at fault."

"No." More tears came.

"You were always a good mother."

Mary's mind was being overrun with memories of her helping out her children, feeding them, and giving them baths. She remembered their smiles as the doctor spoke to her. She remembered cooking cookies for them and watching them cover their faces with chocolate. "Maybe I was a good mother?" she said softly in her mind.

"You are still a good mother to them. You care for them even now. You have never turned your back on them. You always did what a good mother would do. You did your best to protect them, and bad luck doesn't always mean someone is to blame, but I swear to you, Mary, that if there is someone to blame, it is not you."

Mary's arms hung by her side and she wept more. She had tried so hard to help them in all that they did. She helped them with their homework, and read them bedtime stories, and taken them to the park whenever she could. She never shouted at them, or raised a hand to them, she tried so hard to be the best that she could.

"You loved them, and they loved you," he said again.

Mary's mind was still moving, listening and thinking. She had always smiled for them, and played with them, and looked for a good father for them when Gerard died. She had done everything that she could, so why did it hurt so much?

"You are not at fault."

Mary's mind was racing. What was he doing? She cried and cried more and fell into him. He grabbed her and held her up, and she just cried into his shirt.

"You are more than you think, and any mother would be proud to be like you."

She just cried, soaking his nice shirt and tie, but she didn't think about it, and just cried. Her heart felt relieved she was giving up her guilt and although it felt like a weight was lifted, her emotions were on edge. She cried more and more, allowing all of her guilt for her children to come out slowly in the form of water from her eyes. Each tear holding a small amount of her guilt and thoughts of her negligence that was false. One by one the tears ran down her cheeks taking a thought with them, each one. Her heart was in pain, but still the tears took the thoughts away, and, like a pool draining slowly from two small leaks, like those from an eyedropper, her guilt consciousness thoughts drained from her pool of sorrow.

Doctor Ross knew that this was not the end of her treatment, but it was a great step in the right direction. He couldn't be absolutely sure, though, if her crying meant that she had began to believe her innocence or not, but through his experience, her collapsing reaction seemed to show that she had let go of, at least, some of her guilt, and her emotions were boiling over. The doctor spent another fifteen minutes coaxing her as she kept crying in his bosom allowing the water to drip out of her pool and onto him. After the time had passed, Doctor Ross was able to move her back to her chair and set her down.

Mary's mind was still in the wake of emotional disorder. She allowed her mind to let go of its guilt. She had known, for a while, that her guilt could not be completely realistic, but she couldn't bring herself to believe it from her own mouth. "But," she thought to herself. "Why was I able to let go of it, coming from his mouth? I hardly even know him." Her mind was still in shambles and her thinking of how it all happened didn't help her composure any and she wept still. Mary's mind fought not only with the intriguing and unexpected release of guilt, but also with the dilemma of the doctor haunting her. But she put her questions of his credibility on hold after only a moment of thought though; she had more pressing matters pouring, like a cascading waterfall, through and out of her mind.

"I think that you are a very tough person," started the doctor. "You have been through a great deal, but you have survived. I have a new notebook for you to take home, if you want."

She just stared at him, her mind not completely ready to move on to the next subject, but she handed him her latest accomplishment: her notebook. He didn't spend any time reading it, but his eyes widened to see the sheer volume of words that infested the book. It was obviously more than he anticipated.

"The reason I have a new notebook for you, is that I would like to take this one and read it thoroughly. Is that okay?"

"Yes," she said. She felt a little better; he wanted to read what she had written. It wasn't just a useless chore!

"You did a very difficult thing, just a minute ago. It is hard to face one's own doubt."

Mary didn't say anything; she didn't really know what to say or what to think for that matter.

"You want to know something interesting," the doctor started again, but Mary wasn't very interested. "Your brain functions on chemicals and electrical energy. Some chemicals are needed for different thoughts to happen."

Mary still didn't seem very interested. She just thought he was talking mumbo jumbo, but she tried to keep her attention on him since his rapid changes of subject were always present in their discussions.

"Sometimes a lack of certain chemicals or an abundance of other chemicals or a combination of lots of chemicals can make for a person who is very happy, or very depressed, or very tired, or very sleepy, or any other number of problems."

Mary didn't see where he was going with this, but she tried to stay alert though her mind was exhausted with more emotions than she could count.

"So, for years psychiatrists thought that we should simply give a drug that would stabilize the chemical imbalance and that would be it. Luckily, the science of psychology has progressed a bit since then. Now we know, for certain, that the thoughts that you make not only need certain chemicals to function, but in doing so, tell the mind to produce more of those same chemicals. Thus, if you think happy thoughts, then more pleasure filled thoughts could come from the gained chemicals. And, in the same effect, a sad thought produced more chemicals that allowed for more saddening thoughts, or a loss of chemicals necessary for happy thoughts. Do you want to know why I'm telling you all of this Mary?"

"Yea, okay."

"I'm telling you this because we need to change your thinking, so that you can make more of the proper chemicals for your mind."

"I'm confused. You're saying that all I have to do is think happy thoughts and I will become happy. Like the old idea such when you are sad just start smiling and you will feel better?"

"Almost," he replied. "Not only do you have to think the happy thoughts, but you have to realize and understand your negative thinking. You have to be able to know when you are thinking disruptive thoughts. That way you can stop yourself from losing control. The smiling thing only works if you can come to grips with your negative thoughts and then move on to a smile."

"I'm still confused, but I'm guessing that all of this has to do with what you are having me do in these notebooks?"

"Yes, exactly. You spent the last three weeks writing in your notebook about situations or thoughts that make you feel bad. What we need to do is remind you that some problems are easier to solve than it seems, and that you are stronger than you think you are."

"Well I'm not sure about that," she said.

"That is okay. You don't have to be. I will believe it for the both of us for now, but in time, you will believe it again too."

Mary shrugged off the idea; it all seemed so made up. Strange chemicals producing more strange chemicals and all of it leading to sadness or happiness. She didn't know if she was strong; she didn't even know if she was strong enough to be weak. Not to mention the entire trauma that had taken her over in the last hour. It was all too much to digest.

"I know that it will be hard for a while, Mary. I just want you to know, before you leave today," he said as time closed near. "You have done well today, and don't ever forget how strong you had to be to realize that you are not guilty for your children's passing. You were and are a good mother. Don't ever forget it, and if you ever feel that it isn't true, remind yourself of the good things that you did for them, and never the meaningless instances when you were not in control."

Mary just looked at him. She was shocked at what all had happened, and she wasn't sure how she should react. The time came and she walked towards the door. The doctor followed her as she opened the door to see her father sitting in a chair. She left into the waiting area and looked back for just a second to hear Doctor Ross. "Have a good evening, Mary." She took her new notebook with her and got into the car with her father. She didn't want to think of all that had happened in that hour of discussion. The doctor had a way of almost seeing right through her, and it disturbed her just a bit. She forgot the thought and let her mind stop working on the drive home. She stared out the window and looked at the snow in the grass of so many lawns on their way home. The driveways were plowed, but the ground shown white as glue and reflected the sun's rays with color and brightness. Mary peered into the snow and pondered her life for just a moment. The doctor wanted her to realize her negative thoughts. Why? She closed her eyes and leaned her head against the cold glass and just faded her mind away, and for just a second, embraced the warm feeling that came from knowing that she didn't have to be in control of everything all the time. She thought of her father driving her home, and how protected she must be, for he would never allow her to get hurt.

Chapter 11

She went home and went to her bathroom. She turned on the light and saw her bloodshot eyes, her obvious show of her tears, and just looked at herself. She turned on the cold water and put her hands under the flow and splashed her face. The cool sensation seemed to wash away more and more of the pain. The cleansing feeling that she attained from the cool water put some joy in her heart. It was not sustained, though, as she remembered the strain of her day. Mary dried off her face and walked slowly into her room. She pondered existence for a brief moment and stared off into the void that consumed her walls. She lost herself in the small wrinkles of the wall and its lavender covering. After ten minutes of just staring and standing in the same place, she walked over to her window, and looked out to her tree.

She walked back to her vanity and took the wooden chair that was placed at its base. She moved it beside the wall, just under the window. She was just high enough to look out and see her tree as she rested her forearms on the windowsill. She reminisced about her youthful days of just losing herself in the beauty of the tree, and dream of what was to come. Mary decided to do the same on that day. It was night time soon after she got home, but the moonlight lit up the snow at the base of the tree and shone the colors of the rainbow, as the crystals of water made millions of small prisms. She looked into the branches of the trees and took meticulous detailed sights of every small twig that held on tightly to its branch as snow pulled it towards the ground.

"The poor little twig," she said to herself. "Gravity is pulling down so much weight upon it, but it is holding on. Much like me, I guess. I feel like that twig. I'm hardly alive, and being pulled down, but I suppose I'm hanging on as well. I'm not sure why, though. I may not be directly or even indirectly responsible for my children, but I still don't feel like I have a reason to live. Poor little twig, hold on. Hold on."

Mary focused her attention, once again, to the world back in her room and realized that she was hungry. She went downstairs to find that her mother was cooking some supper- pork chops- she could smell it from the stairs. Mary took a seat in a reclining chair with its partner a few feet away and holding her father. He was watching the local news, and looked over to her with another one of his intrigued faces. She looked at him for a moment, and then turned her head away towards the television. She could tell that her father was happy just to see her downstairs and eating dinner. He felt that she was getting better, and that is what frightened Mary more than most things. She knew in her heart that she was far from a happy person and she didn't want to give them a false impression that her newfound energy was her illness fading away. She didn't want to let them down, and she didn't even feel like being happy yet. With that in mind, Mary just stared at the television.

Before long, dinner was ready and Mary proceeded to the table. She did not speak to her parents and she tried not to look at them. She could feel that they wanted to hear how her sessions were going, but she didn't want to talk with them. Did she have to? Was it inevitable? Mary kept her head down as her parents made small talk waiting to break into a conversation with Mary. They hadn't had the chance to talk with her in months, and like parents missing their children as they are away, Mary's parents yearned to converse with her.

"How are your sessions going?" Mary's father chanced.

"They are okay," replied Mary quickly with her face down toward her plate.

"Do you like Doctor Ross?" asked her mother.

"He is fine."

"Well," started her father again. "We are glad to see that you are eating with us again tonight." Mary was silent.

"Christmas is coming up soon," said her mother. "Is there anything that you want special? We have a couple gifts, but we were wondering if you wanted anything big, since we haven't gotten you much in the last few years."

"There is nothing that I want."

"Well, if you think of anything, be sure to tell us."

"Okay," she responded, telling them just enough so as not to say a single unnecessary word. Mary finished with her meal and excused herself from the table. She was tired, but not sleepy at all. She had spent so much time sleeping in the last few months that was becoming too much of a habit. She went upstairs and just sat on her bed thinking and relaxing. Nine o'clock came, but she was still wide-awake with her mind moving. She had a couple of crying bouts, but for the most part she just didn't want to go to sleep. Midnight came and the same energy still surrounded her. By then though, she tried to go to sleep but she laid in bed tossing and turning, her mind still racing after any thought. She felt as though she took a caffeine pill. Two in the morning came, and still she was awake. Her body was exhausted, and her mind was exhausted, but it kept moving her, forcing her to react on the day's events. She was beginning to feel that she was losing control of her own mind. Four in the morning came, seven hours after her normal bedtime, and she was too exhausted from tumbling around so much. Her mind gave up and she slept.

She awoke the next morning, bright and early, at eight. She was devastatingly tired, but she was awake none the less. "Why? What is happening to me?" Mary got up out of bed and looked around her room, and fixed her eyes on her clock. "Why?" she pondered. "Maybe I'm thinking too much or something, but I don't know how to turn it off."

She made her way to the shower, her thighs and arms aching as she walked. Her body had not been through much physical stress in the last few days, but the fatigue was there, so what was she to do. It might have had something to do with her growing need for an abundance of sleep, or the one night's lack, but that was a long thought. She arched her back and yawned. She could feel every muscle in her body telling her that she should go to sleep, but her mind was wide-awake. "How could this be," she kept asking herself.

Mary forgot the thought and tried to go about her day, not that it was so exciting in the first place.

Mary spent some more time writing in her notebook that day. She spent over one hour writing, not only about her thoughts, but what she thought about her thoughts. She was still overcome quite easily by the visions of her dying family and her self-doubt, but she wanted to write down as much as possible.

She spent a lot of time when she was younger running in races, playing soccer, and playing tennis. She was very athletic in her youth and she always did great in school. She wasn't always the fastest or the best, and she definitely wasn't the smartest of all the other students, but she tired hard in everything that she did. When she was tired in sports she willed herself to do well. The cliché, "When the going gets tough, the tough get going," was more than her way of thinking-it was her lifestyle. She wasn't very popular, but that didn't bother her. She would run her races and play her games, and although fatigue and sheer pain would plague her on these adventures, she would literally bite her own lip and press on. When she was working for a class, writing an essay, or doing research, she did not give into temptation of television or the lure of the phone easily. She worked hard in her schooling, to do well. She had worked hard all throughout her life, and the courage of her youth and the rest of her life had been dormant in the last few months. It was pushed back with hurt feelings and negative thinking. She could not believe that she could be strong, but with the reassurance from the doctor, the feeling was trying to emerge. She would not let it show its form though. She wasn't sure if the doctor's glee was true, or if it was an act and she couldn't believe herself that she was capable of doing well, but her old lifestyle and thoughts kept poking at her none the less. Almost as if she wanted to believe, but just couldn't find it in herself.

Her day went by slowly as she thought to herself and argued constantly. She was slowly losing her belief that she was at fault for her children's death, but she fought herself on every other aspect of her life. Was she a good enough wife? Was she a good enough daughter? Was the doctor just playing her along? Her mind was not content and her tired body ached. She could do nothing but argue with her body the same that she argued with her mind, telling it that it was no good, and that it should be stronger. She paced, as she normally did, starring aimlessly at the walls and remembering her youth. Lunch was ready near noon and she went downstairs to join her family. Mary did not feel like talking very much, but she no longer wanted to feel guilty for her mother having to drag her lunch up to her room, and so she decided to join them and put the burden on her shoulders.

Mary had lunch and dinner and some breakfasts with her family for the entire week before the following Wednesday found its way into her life again. She was not really happy to be going back to see the doctor, but unlike the past four times, she was not scared or unhappy with the idea. She had grown indifferent about the subject and all its meaning, almost like a vaccination shot. She knew that it had to be done and not to waste her time fearing it, Mary just simply accepted it as part of her new life.

The lunch before the afternoon though brought Mary into difficult thinking though. It was December the twenty-first that afternoon. Christmas was on the upcoming Sunday. "Mary," her mother asked her. "I know that you are tired a lot, and it is tough to go outside since it is so cold, but I wanted to see if you would like to join us at church Christmas Eve."

"No. Not with all of those people!" Mary responded shortly and almost coldly.

"Why not, dear? What is wrong with the people?"

"I don't want them to see me!" answered Mary with a slightly raised voice.

"Why not, dear?"

"I just don't want to. Can we drop it?"

"Okay."

They finished their lunch and Mary went back to her room to wait and ponder. "Where am I going right now? Do I still have a purpose here?" The time did come after a few hours and Mary bundled herself up to go to the office. Her ride with her father was silent as usual, and her father found a place to wait just as he did the last time. He sat in the waiting room and read a few magazines, and Mary walked towards the open door, with its seemingly endless invitations spewing from it.

Mary walked in and was greeted by the ever-smiling doctor. "Hello, Mary. How are you today?"

"I don't know."

"Why do you say that?"

"Because my parents want me to go with them to church on Christmas Eve." Mary finished and casually sat down in her chair. She almost seemed comfortable, but Mary would never admit that to herself.

"Why is that such a tough thing to do?" he asked taking his seat as well.

"Because of all the people."

"Why are you afraid of them?"

"I'm not afraid of them," she snapped. "I just don't want them asking me a lot of questions about where I've been, what's wrong with me, why I'm crazy, and other things."

"Do you really think that they would ask those questions on Christmas Eve?"

"Well, they will surely ask me where I've been. What would I have to tell them, that I'm crazy and I've been in therapy?"

"No. You could tell them the truth," he responded.

"That is the truth!"

"I don't think you really believe that. You could tell them that you have been taking your children's passing pretty hard and that you have been very upset about that." Mary didn't respond. "I'm sure that they would completely understand."

"But what if they don't?"

"I'm sorry?" he asked.

"What if they ask me a lot of questions about where I've been, and I don't answer fast enough, and then they think that I'm crazy, and they all start talking about me."

"Whoa. Do you see where your mind took you?"

"What?" she asked.

"You just assumed that if you didn't answer quickly enough then they would think that you are crazy. Why wouldn't they just think that you are still upset?"

"I don't know, because people like to pass judgment and they like to gossip. A crazy lady is a lot more fun to gossip about."

"Okay, so let's say that, on the off chance, they do gossip about you, and they all think that you are crazy, although we have no proof that they would. Why would that bother you?"

"Because I don't want people to think that I'm crazy!"

"But you aren't crazy," he rebutted.

"Well, I know that, but they don't."

"They also don't know that you are. They don't know one way or the other, but let's stay with this for a second. Okay, say that these people do start gossiping and the entire town starts thinking that you are crazy. Would that be so bad?"

"Yes!" Mary was baffled, how could that *not* be important, maybe the doctor was crazy. He seemed so strange every moment that she found herself in his office.

"Why would that be so bad? Most of the people don't even know who you are, and you don't know many of them yourself. It wouldn't be like your friends are thinking that you are crazy."

"But what if they do start to think that I'm crazy?"

"Would that be so bad?"

"God, yes! Are you sure that you aren't the crazy one!" Mary threw her hands in the air trying to understand this "doctor."

Doctor Ross chuckled for just a bit, and Mary even released a smile. "I'm just saying," he continued. "If any one of your friends believes a rumor that you are crazy, then that person really isn't your friend."

"How could that *not* be a bad thing?"

"Well because, with all of the time we spend in our lives getting along with other people, and the tremendous amount of time that we spend with our friends, with one swift rumor you could weed out who really is your friend and who really isn't. And then you could spend your time more appropriately."

"But I would be losing a friend," she countered.

"If that friend believes a rumor, then they were never a friend to begin with. All you would lose is useless baggage."

Mary almost laughed at the though. This man really was crazy, but he had a point. "I just don't know."

"I'm sure though, that if you go, that it will be tough. You will have to make pointless chit chat with people that you don't really like, and you will have to deal with people staring at you."

"Why would they be staring?" she asked.

"Well, no one in town has seen you since your children passed, and then all of a sudden you are there in church."

"What would they think?" she asked.

"Don't worry about what they would think."

"Why not? It is important to know if people are talking about you."

"It is?" the doctor questioned.

"Yes! That way you can know what kind of an impression that you are giving off."

"Oh, so now you are worried about whether or not you will impress them?"

"What, no? What? Stop trying to turn my words around!"

"You are worried about their impressions on you. We all do it. We all worry about what other people think, but I'll give you a hint. The happiest people in the world, don't care what other people think about them."

"Well, that is easy for you to say. You're not crazy," she said.

"Neither are you, and I want you to do something for me. Do you think that you can?"

"I don't know. That depends on what you want me to do?"

"I want you to stop saying that you are crazy, because you are not crazy, and you know that you aren't. So I want you to try and think only positive thoughts about yourself, and stop saying any stereotypical word for a person in therapy, including crazy, loony-toon, nut job, nut ball, nut case, funny farm, and at any point time considered 'out of one's mind'." His attempt to lighten the mood of the conversation worked and Mary saw the humor in what he said. But, even through his levity, she could also tell that he had required a serious response from her.

Mary considered the question for a bit, but like a child folding under a large authority figure she gave in. "Fine."

"Now, back to the church. Things like this can help define who we are. This can help you realize who you are now. If you have the courage to go, then you can reassure yourself one more time that you are strong enough to face your fears."

"Yea, but I don't know if I can."

"I know that you can. I know that it will be difficult, but you strike me as the type of person that doesn't give up too easily."

"I don't know," said Mary.

"Nor do I. We will just leave that thought at that. Now, what else has been on your mind?"

Doctor Ross and Mary talked for a while more, and Ross made it a point to reprimand her every time she used the word crazy to define her state of mind.

"Mary," said the doctor. "I read over you notebook, and it was very elaborate. I commend you on your workmanship, but now we must discuss the meanings in the notebook."

"Okay," she responded.

"Let us think about why a person feels bad. You know that I told you about the chemicals in the brain and how they are effected by our thoughts. Back on that subject, we are going to discuss where our mind takes us when we are worried or sad or happy or energetic, any number of feelings. Most people have thoughts of their own death from time to time, it is one of those things that we have to come to grips with, but where our mind takes us from there is very important."

"I'm not sure what you mean."

"Well, the thought of dying is not necessarily a negative thought-it is just life. But many times a person will think about their own death and then visualize it happening. Then they visualize the pain and suffering that might come from it, and then a person may be anxious about what happens to their friends or their family, and the person can become worried about that also, and it all came from a simple thought."

"I think that I know what you mean."

"Say a person isn't sure if they locked their front door to their house. They may worry that someone could come into the house, and steal their furniture, and then they might get hurt, attacked. Those are situations that, yes, could happen, but a person that thinks situations like that a lot will begin to believe that they are more probable than they really are."

"You lost me again," said Mary.

"Are you afraid of lightning?" asked the doctor.

"No."

"Then does it seem strange that a person would not leave their house if they knew that lightning *might* strike him since he saw some dark clouds in the sky. He could be so afraid that he wouldn't leave his house, take a shower, or stand anywhere near an outlet. Does that sound strange?"

"Yes!"

"That is the way a person might act if they were deathly afraid of lightning. Do you have an idea of why they are so afraid of it?"

"No."

"It is all in their thought processes. They are not only afraid of lightning, but also many times when they see lightning or clouds, they see themselves getting hit by the lightning and that frightens them. They imagine themselves getting hurt, and it frightens them so much that they don't want to take the chance of walking outside on a cloudy day. They imagine the clouds forming right above them out of nowhere, and single them out and strike him."

"That seems strange."

"Millions of people in this world are afraid of very real dangers: plane crashes, disease, lightning, spiders, closed areas, and heights. And although many of those instances have very real danger, the chances are low that say a spider will creep on you in your sleep and bite you and you would die. The truth is that there are hardly any spiders in the world that could do that, and almost none here in the United States. But when a person sees himself or herself getting bitten in his or her own mind, they believe that it is more probable than it really is. The major problem is that he will keep having the thoughts, maybe even one hundred times a day. Every time that he has that thought, his mind thinks it is more likely to happen to him."

"I think that I'm understanding a little bit," explained Mary.

"You want to know something else that is interesting?"

"Sure, I guess." Mary couldn't help but think that this man talked too much.

"The phobias that I am talking about and the depression that hurts you are very similar. They are both caused by the mind turning something that is small into something that is very big, or something that doesn't matter into something that is necessary for life. But I don't want you to think that your children passing is a menial occurrence, but I do want you to know that it is related."

"But I thought depression was like a chemical imbalance or something," inquired Mary.

"It is."

"Then how can phobias and depressions be the same?"

"Because, thoughts produce chemicals. The mind can become unbalanced if a person has too many negative thought patterns."

"So, what are you saying about me? That I don't think right?"

"In a manner of speaking, yes." Mary frowned at the thought. "But it isn't as simple as that. Say a person's thinking is walking on a path, you mind might have just stepped off to take a look at the trees along side, and got lost along the way. We just have to get you to the right path."

"Okay?"

"And I want to tell you something else before you leave here today."

"Sure."

"The best thing about therapy without taking pills everyday or shock therapy or strange reversions to your past is that when we get you to the path again, you won't wander off as easily anymore. In fact, most of those things that would take you off the path are easily avoidable. And if you want to, not only will you rarely feel depression, but also you won't easily be anxious about things that you can't control. You will probably never have a phobia, and you will be generally happier. All without pills."

"It all sounds so good, Doc, but it seems hard to accomplish."

"It is hard. You can't rely on anything but yourself and me to help guide you. But the strength that you will gain, if you stick with it, will be unmatched by anyone staying out of depression with pills. I know that this seems impossible. That is why I am here. But I am just a guide and I'm useless if you don't walk with me."

"But why did you tell me all of this, Doc?"

"I told you all of this to reassure you that there is light at the end of the tunnel, and sometimes just understanding the possibilities can help us along in life."

Mary nodded and stood up. Her hour had passed ten minutes earlier and she left with a smile creeping onto her face. The doctor seemed to have so many good ideas, and he seemed to have answers for everything. Could everything that he said be true? It seemed so hard to imagine. Only time would tell. Mary left and her mind was given something else to chew on for another week.

She finished up her day in her room as always thinking more and more about if she would go to the church on Christmas Eve. She was afraid of what the people would think of her. She didn't want her peers to pity her or say how wretched she must feel. True, she was in pain, but she didn't want others to see it. Like a dog that hides when it knows that it is going to die, she didn't want others to see her in a disturbed state, and if they did, her pride and dignity might take a loss. She wanted to remain strong in public. But they wouldn't expect her to be strong. "All the more reason why I should be strong," she thought to herself. "But what if I'm not as strong, and I don't surprise them with my strength. Then they will think exactly what they had been thinking-that I am hurt. But I am hurt! But we don't want them to know that. "Why not?" Because you are strong! Am I? Yes. I'm confused again."

Mary was tired, and her body told her more and more. The last week was not one of much sleep. She just could not get her mind into a comfortable place, and now, with this new information from Doctor Ross, how could she sleep that night? He seemed so optimistic, like what he had was a cure to so many tough and seemingly impossible problems. What if he was right, and he did have a cure? How could that be, though? It seemed logical enough. Mary paced until three in the morning and found a way to fall asleep moments later in bed. Her dreams were few and far between lately also, maybe because she didn't spend much time asleep. That night she did not remember any dreams, and woke up at eight in the morning. The Thursday air seemed little different than any other days, but it held great meaning. It was one day closer to her Saturday trauma. Would she go? Should she go? Mary looked out her cold window and stared at her tree pondering the thought of dealing with so many people, but her body did not allow her any peace as it shouted to her in fatigue. "Why did it have to be so cold? I thought we had global warming, what happened?" Mary shook off her thoughts and decided that a warm shower would help her out. She enjoyed the warm water of her shower and tried to forget her day and her problem that would soon be upon her. What was with that moment that we try to hold onto so strongly? Later there will be difficulties so we cling to the present safety and comfort. Maybe we would lose our minds if we didn't.

She got out of the shower and talked herself out of going with her parents on the seemingly dreadful Christmas Eve. "I shouldn't have to go. I haven't been out in a while around other people, sure, but there are ways that I can slowly get back into the groove. I could take it slowly and just have company over or something like that."

"But whom would you invite?"

"That doesn't matter, as long as it isn't the entire church! Yes, I won't go with them, and my parents will understand. They just want to try and help me, and I will explain to them that I shouldn't start drastically."

"But wouldn't that be giving up?"

"No! Just because we are going to take it slow doesn't mean that we are going to give up."

"Okay then, that sounds good."

Mary dressed herself with a sense of relief and reassurance about the next few days in her life. She had decided not to do the hard thing and was relieved that she would not have to put forth the effort of dealing with so many nosy people. Throughout the day, though, she could feel herself trying to second guess her choice, but in every instance, she found a way to convince herself to take the easy route. Luckily, her parents did not bring up the subject on that day, and Mary was able to go about her day without any added worries that could form from a single conversation with them.

"It would be too hard to go to the church with that many people," Mary kept reassuring herself. By the end of the day she had doubted and reassured herself nearly fifty times. She knew that part of her was urging her to do the hard thing, to suck it up, but she could not find the strength in her heart.

Mary went to her bed near eleven at night. She didn't know why she was on her way there. She was unable to get much sleep in the last week or so, and she definitely didn't get to sleep before two or three in the morning, but she just kept moving. She undid her hair and put her nightgown on and jumped into the cold covers. She shivered for just a bit, but the heavy blankets began to get warm, and for the first time in a week, she was able to simply sleep. Her eyes took no time to fall. She didn't know why sleep came so easily, but just as her body shut itself down, and just before she lost consciousness of the situation, she could feel her mind letting go of a worry, and perhaps that was the reason for her ease.

The next two days up until an hour before church on Saturday night went by quickly with reasonable sleep for Mary, and no major breakdowns. But it was that night that she had been dreading that brought forth anxiety. Mary knew that she did not want to go, but she didn't want to fight her parents about it, and she worried that she would have to fight them, and that she would lose her temper. And if she lost her temper, they might throw her out. So she worried. One hour until they were to be at the church, her mother came to her door. The door was open and Mary could see her mother dressed in a black dress with nice shoes and her hair done, and looking the best that she could.

"Mary, will you be coming with us tonight," noticing that she was not dressed, just in jeans and a shirt.

"No, I don't think so, Mom."

"Why not, dear? It is only an hour?"

Mary could feel the frustration coming, but she tried to hold it back since her mother was not pressing her. "I just don't feel up to it. There would just be too many people." Mary was convinced that her excuse would work well, but her mother would not give up easily.

"There won't be that many people that you know there anyway. You know Christmas Eve. Everyone comes!"

"I may not know them, but they all know who I am. I don't want to deal with them asking me questions and staring at me."

"I don't think that anyone would do that," explained Mary's mother.

"I just don't feel up to it, okay Mom? I want to take my assimilation back into the normal society slowly."

"Okay dear. We will be back around eight thirty," she said with a smile. Her smile seemed endless. Whether she should or not, her mother always found a way to smile at her. She was stunned for a moment afterwards thinking of her mother's smile. Her parents had been so great to her at every turn in her life. Why did she have so many bad feelings against them? She shook her head and tried to forget the thought.

Mary spent the rest of her night sitting in her room worrying about disappointing her parents. "Why didn't I just go? I should have gone! Would it have been that hard to do that for them? I'm a lousy daughter. Here they have worked so hard, and I act like I've gotten better, but I still feel lousy and I won't even make the effort to go to the church with them. I'm weak and dumb! I hate myself!" Mary cried.

Mary's tears did not end, nor did her thoughts of her parents disapproval, or her own lack of self worth, until she heard her parents come in through the front door. Mary, ashamed from her crying, ran to her bathroom and shut the door quickly so that she could wash her face off before they would have a chance to see her. She turned on the cold water and splashed herself in the face. Again and again she splashed. For a minute straight, she splashed and tried to hold back more tears, but they could not be stopped, she kept crying. She felt horribly guilty for not going with her parents, and she sobbed more. She nearly wailed as she threw open the door and ran downstairs to her parents. They were instantly stunned to see her running to them with tears streaming down her face. She fell on her knees at her mother's feet and cried so loudly that it hurt her head and throat.

"I'm so sorry that I didn't go with you Mom. I'm so sorry," she said again. Her mother and father both kneeled down, both still in shock at her behavior, and Mary buried her face into her father's chest. "I'm so sorry Daddy, for wasting your money and not getting better. I'm just still sad!" she said bursting into more tears.

"No, no, no. Don't worry Honey, it is okay. You can go out whenever you are ready. You are never a waste of my money! You are never a waste of anything that we have or are. You are my daughter; all that I have is for you. We love you so much."

Her mother and father held on to her tightly as she cried more and more, and they realized that her depression was making her feel overly guilty, but they were sympathetic and nearly cried themselves. Mary was unable to think that she hadn't hurt her parents and she cried for an hour with her father sitting right there with her. Mary couldn't understand what was happening in her mind, but she was finally able to get to her feet and her father walked her to her room as she fell into bed. She was still dressed, but she did not care, Mary just cried into her pillow a bit, but was asleep in just minutes; her body exhausted and her mind consumed with turmoil.

The next morning came and Mary's mother woke her up at ten in the morning. "Come on downstairs, Mary," she said. "I made some hot chocolate and your father has a nice warm fire started."

Mary complied and got out of bed, taking a few moments to ponder why her mother woke her up, but she soon realized that it was Christmas. She noticed that she had slept in her clothes, though, and she felt groggy. She undressed and put on a pair of sweats and a sweatshirt. Her toes were cold so she decided to put on two pairs of socks and she made her way downstairs.

She walked into the living room to notice the big tree stuffed with ornaments that she hadn't even seen since it went up. She took a seat on the floor near the fireplace and stared at the flames jump up and down, and dance like music played for them. Her mother brought her a steaming cup of hot chocolate and Mary enjoyed it, but felt guilty for not getting them any presents. She hadn't left the house for shopping, but Mary was simply too tired to worry about crying over it. She finished her cup at the same time her mother and father took a seat near her, and handed her a small box.

Mary looked at it as her parents looked on huddled together, her father with his arm around his wife, and Mary took a small moment to remember her lost husband on their first Christmas together. The moment passed before she could cry from it and she focused her attention once more on the small box in her hands. She took off the red and green wrapping paper and found a black box underneath the paper. She noticed that it was a jewelry box, but she opened it to see what it hid. She found a platinum lock-it with a heart shape like most. She opened the heart to find two small pictures. One was a picture of her and her late husband, and the other was a picture of her two little girls in their Easter dresses from the year before. Mary burst into tears.

"I'm sorry," said her mother. "We didn't want to make you cry again. I know that you still think about Gerard, so we thought that it would be okay, but I'm sorry that we made you sad."

"No, no, Mom; Dad. I couldn't ask for anything better. Thank you so much," she said getting up to hug them. Mary's heart was filled with conflicting emotions. The pictures made her remember that they were gone, but she could feel the joy of her life when she looked at the pictures. She cried tears, not only of sadness, but with a bit of happiness mixed into them. "I'm going to go and put it on," she said.

Mary went to the bathroom and looked into the mirror. The necklace was made for one length. Mary took off her shirt and hooked the necklace together in the back. She had found a way to stop crying for just a moment, to look at the necklace. She saw as the heart rested itself on top of her own heart. The length was just perfect. It rested on her naked bosom, and although the metal was cold against her skin, she couldn't move her eyes. Gerard had given her a necklace when they were first dating, but she took it off when he died. Mary thought to herself that this was the perfect replacement for it. Mary just stared off into the mirror, forgetting about the chill in the air and seemed happy for that minute or two.

The rest of the day Mary seemed to find happiness in her present, but the more exhilaration she got out of her gift, the more guilty she felt about not getting her parents anything. Near the evening after a large meal of turkey, Mary went to her room to cry and feel guilty about all of the things she had failed at in the last few days. Although her parents did not believe so, Mary felt as though she did not meet her parents' expectations by not going to church, and multiplied with the guilt of no Christmas presents, Mary had her emotions filled to the brim. Not only did her crying take up most of her evening, but writing it all down into her notebook was a chore that took up another hour of her life. By the end of it all, she was exhausted and wanted nothing more than to go to sleep.

Mary found her way to bed, and before she could get to sleep, she wondered about the doctor. Did he have a family? What was his family like? She had never noticed a ring on his finger, but she was not looking for it either. She made a note to herself to ask him how his Christmas went. She had never thought of the Doctor's life up until that moment. Was she losing her negative presumptions of him or was this some strange attraction? She knew that it could not be the latter and dismissed the thought, and some how her mind found its way back to her own dreary life. Although she had failed her parents, Mary promised herself that she would be nice to the doctor to help make up for some of her shortcomings. Mary could take her thinking no longer and the Sandman caught up with her.

Chapter 12

The next few days went by without any major complications in Mary's life. She enjoyed watching the snow fall down the day after Christmas, and she loved to see each flake hit a branch of the wilted tree and either stick or slide off and head for the prevailing ground. The white haze of snowflakes came down and mystified Mary. She was completely hypnotized with the constant flow of beauty. Like water coming down from a waterfall the flakes made their way down, but almost in slow motion as they coasted to their destination. And although the ten minutes or so that Mary could lose herself looking out the window and enjoy nature, she could not escape all of the emotions she had accumulated in the last forty-eight hours. She almost felt eager to see the doctor. Doctor Ross was her outlet now. She was beginning to feel that she could talk with him about a lot of things. She still felt that he might be a little off also, but he was a good ear, and although he made her angry or sad or mad, she felt that maybe he was on the right track with her.

So for Mary the two days slowly went by as she waited more and more to talk with the doctor about everything that had happened. She needed clarity of mind and clairvoyance of the actions she should take. As the Wednesday afternoon approached slowly, her mind went from an indifferent thought about seeing the doctor into a near yearning to get her thoughts off of her chest. She waited and waited, and after many pages were written in her notebook, the afternoon finally came. She approached the door into his office and mixed feelings came over her. "Will he think that I'm crazy if I ask him about all of my feelings for the last few days? No, that is his job. I don't know." Mary swallowed the thought and walked through the door.

"Hello Mary, and Merry Christmas!" responded the doctor as she walked into the room.

"Merry Christmas to you too, Doctor."

"Please take a seat. How are you doing today?" he inquired with his usual cheerful tone.

"Well, I have a lot to talk with you about today."

"I can't wait, where would you like to start?" he asked.

"Well, to start with, the fact that I didn't go to church on Christmas Eve with my parents."

"Okay, how did that turn out?"

"Bad."

"How so?" he asked.

"Well, I felt so guilty for not going that I cried for an hour or so after they left and when they got home I just cried more and more. I apologized to them, but I cried myself to sleep afterwards."

"So you felt guilty for not going with them. Why did you feel guilty?"

"Because I thought that I should have been strong enough to go, and I thought I owed my father for all of these sessions that he is paying for. I should have been strong for him."

"Before we put blame anywhere or talk of too many ways it could have gone, let's talk about the reasons why you didn't go. What do you think was your core reason for not going?"

"I guess that I just wanted to try a few people at first, before I got submersed in them, you know?"

"I understand," explained the doctor. "That is a good idea. You shouldn't feel guilty about that."

"I know, but, well I don't know."

"Is there anything else?"

"Yes, well, I don't know. Well, I felt like I told myself that as a cop out for not going. I knew that I probably could stand the people, but I just wanted the easy route."

"I understand. The easy road is taken more often than the hard, but in your case, the easy route may have been the right route. Instead of being overwhelmed and becoming possibly more adverted to people, you decided not to try your luck. And although you may know that you had the strength to go on, a few people at first is probably the safest way to go."

"So you are saying that I shouldn't feel guilty?" she asked.

"That is correct. And if you chose the correct route then there is no reason that your parents could not be satisfied with your progress, because in the act of making a conscious decision about your emotional well being, you show progress. So what else has been on your mind?"

Mary seemed overwhelmed at first by his rather lengthy explanation, but enough of the explanation set in to continue, and so she moved onto the next thought. "I have another problem though," started Mary. "My parents gave me a terrific Christmas gift." Mary pulled out her necklace, in a quick and excited motion almost like a child, and opened the heart so that the doctor could see her family.

"Those are some good looking kids you have there," he responded.

"Thank you, but can you see the problem?"

"What is the problem?"

"This great gift made me cry both because I was sad, but also because it made me so happy, and I didn't get them anything for Christmas."

"And I bet you felt guilty about that also?" he asked.

"Yes, and the more happy I was about my gift from them, the more guilty that I felt for not getting them anything that made them as happy as they had made me."

"I see. Go on."

"There isn't much else, but I just cried a lot about that too. Is it okay for me to be crying so much?"

"It is perfectly all right," explained the doctor. "When mourning it is fine to cry, just try not to cry about something unrelated to your children, but either way, be sure to drink plenty of water, but let's get back to your guilt for your gift."

"Okay."

"How many times have you left your house since your children have passed, to do anything, but come to my office?"

"I haven't."

"So you have had no time, either alone or with them, to shop for a gift for them?"

"That is correct."

"So why feel bad? You haven't had any time or energy to go and buy them a gift. I'm sure they don't mind."

"But I should have. I didn't leave, I've been in my house, feeling sorry for myself and not getting a job. I'm such a horrible daughter."

"No you are not a horrible daughter. And I'm not sure that you believe that simply feeling sorry for yourself has kept you inside for that time."

"I don't know. I still feel like I'm no good."

"Have you felt sad that your children died?"

"Well of course!"

"Okay, and do you think that your sadness has effected your mood a little bit, or even your view of yourself?"

"I'm sure it has."

"Okay, and we have already established that you are not at fault for your children's death. Right?"

"Right," she responded with perplexity in thought.

"So if you are not at fault for their death, and their death caused your sadness, and your sadness kept you from wanting to leave the house, and that fear of leaving kept you from buying any gifts, then how could you be at fault for not getting them gifts?"

"I don't know," Mary thought about the question. She pondered it in her mind for some time. "I still think that I should have given them something."

"You gave them your presence."

"Oh, big deal!"

"You never needed a gift from your daughters. Why would your parents want one from you?"

"Because I'm an adult."

"An adult who has suffered tremendously, and the strength that she does spend, she spends in the one thing that your parents really wanted you to do. And that is come to therapy. As far as I can tell, every time that you come here, you are giving them another gift," he responded trying desperately to reassure her of her own worth.

"I think you may be looking to far into all of that Doc."

"Well, I am a shrink," he responded with a laugh. His smiling face and his joke made Mary smile. It shocked Mary. She was not used to smiling. "But, okay. No more analyzing on that point, but can you see how your guilt may be there for no logical reason? Whenever you face an assumption, always ask yourself if there is any proof to back up the thought. And then be sure that it is substantial and not coincidental."

"Okay."

"I want you to try and think about the situation every time that you feel guilty about something. Sometimes you may be at fault, but a lot of times, you may not be completely to blame, and sometimes you may not be to blame at all. So make a note to yourself to think about every aspect leading up to the transgression that made you feel bad."

"Okay," she responded. "I think that I can handle that."

"This is the base for all that we do. If we watch our thinking then its ability to control us is weakened."

"I have a question for you, Doctor," announced Mary.

"Okay."

"Do you have a family?"

"I have a wife and a son and a daughter."

"What are their names?"

"Why do you ask?" questioned the doctor.

"I'm just curious," said Mary.

"My wife's name is Charlotte. My son's name is Daniel, and my daughter's name is Courtney."

Mary didn't have anything else to say for some reason. She had been curious and she was wondering herself why she asked him about them for any reason beyond curiosity, but she seemed to be stopped for the second. The odd silence was quickly broken by the sound of another question from the doctor.

"When do you plan to interact with that small number of people?"

"You mean, instead of a large group? I don't know, I didn't think about it."

"Every Saturday I have a small group of patients get together to talk about what bothers them and just sit around chatting in a room, or we go for a walk in the park; it varies from week to week. It is kind of like group therapy, but it is more like a group of people just relaxing and talking, but I do moderate to enforce positive thinking. It is likely that they will ask you questions about your children though. Would you consider the group regardless?"

"I don't really feel like talking to other people about this yet," she explained.

"Okay, then how about this? Tomorrow I am going to go to the gym. How would you feel if you went with me and we just walked around the indoor track for only as far as you do would like and then we would come right back? Most likely, you wouldn't have to converse with anyone, but it would give you a good chance just to be in a small public place."

"I don't know."

"I will be with you the entire time, and we can leave at any moment that you feel uncomfortable."

"I-I-I. Okay, I guess. But you have to promise me that if anyone starts drilling me with questions, that you will step in." Mary felt strange putting herself in his hands like that. She wasn't sure if that would be such a good idea. This man seemed on the verge of his own mental episode.

"I will watch out for tough questions."

"Okay, I will do that then," Mary summoned without even thinking. The words just seemed to slip out of her mouth involuntarily.

"That is good," started Doctor Ross. "I want to go over a few things before tomorrow though. There will not be that many people there, but since it is the only gym in town, there will be a few people that know your situation. That fear, which you have of people staring at you, might just happen. Do you think that you can handle a few people, as long as it is not a large group?"

"I think so," Mary said. "I don't know."

"If lately you have had a need to prove something to yourself, this will be a good step."

The rest of the session went by without any major provocation of Mary's emotions, and she was able to leave without too much in her mind to fight with. She wasn't sure if she should look forward to the next day. She was going to have to deal with all of those people, although she liked the idea of the doctor being with her. She tried to keep an open mind about it as she went to sleep that night. Doctor Ross told her that he would be there at noon, so she would have to set her alarm. Her sleeping was so erratic that she could not be sure of waking at the right time. Mary put her head on top of her pillow and rested. The relaxation made her feel better about the day to come, but it drew closer every moment, and there wasn't anything that she could do about it. It was almost like she was on a train, and in the horizon she could see its destination, but no matter how slow the train would move, the view was getting larger and larger. "That isn't a bad thing though. No? We are going out in public. What if they stare at you, what if they know what happened to you and you break down in public. You will look like a damn fool. It isn't like I have much of a choice now either way; he is coming one way or the other. Fine then!"

Mary tricked her mind into thinking about something different, and she was able to lose herself in the darkness and quickly fell asleep. Her mind was still working though, as she woke up at eight in the morning, two hours early. She was feeling anxious about the on coming stares from strangers. "What if I can't handle this? That is what the doctor is for. What if he isn't good enough? What if we both lose control at some overly nosy woman that won't go away? I can just see her now, completely obsessed with other people's lives because she isn't happy with her own. Damn people. I can do this. Can I? I'm not sure, but I know that I can do good enough so that the doctor could still help me, even if he isn't as good as he thinks. But what if he's not? I can be strong enough! Can I? I'm not sure if I can handle the work. Be strong. I'm tired. You are not tired; you are just worried. You can do this! I hope so."

Mary took her shower, but try as she might; her mind did not let her relax. But, the time did pass. Noon found its way to her house, and moments after the large grandfather clock in the living room pounded on twelve o'clock, a knock was heard from the door. The doctor was punctual, and Mary's mother was at the door very quickly.

"Well hello, Doctor," began the cheerful and smiling lady. "Please come in, come in. How are you today?"

"Very well, thank you," replied the doctor with a smile on his face as usual.

Moments after Mary heard the door open she forced herself to walk out of her room, down the hall, and to the stairs. As Mary walked down the stairs she noticed that the doctor was dressed up nice as usual, and Mary was somewhat confused at his garb since they were on their way to the gym. "I didn't think that you would dress up for the gym," said Mary.

"Oh, I'm sorry," began Doctor Ross. "Since we are probably only going to do some walking I didn't bother changing, but if it makes you feel uncomfortable, I don't mind changing."

"No, it will be fine," explained Mary.

"Doctor, I'm so happy that you are taking Mary out!" shouted her mother. "You don't know how long she has been cooped up in here. She needs this."

"Mom!" exclaimed the vexed and irritable Mary.

"I wish that we could stay, Mrs. Montgomery, but I am on a restricted time schedule, if you don't mind us leaving?"

"No, no, that will be fine Doctor. Come by some time for dinner. We would love to have you."

"Yes, that would be nice," he stated. "We will have to work something out." With that, the two quickly left and headed out to the car. Doctor Ross opened her door for her to his new Saab and he followed in suit.

"Thank you," began Mary as the car left its spot.

"For what?"

"For getting us out of there before my mother had a chance to humiliate me any more!"

"I understand, my mother is the same way. I think most mothers are," he said smiling.

"I mean, it is one thing if I say something to someone about my life, but she has no right to give out personal information like that!" announced Mary.

"I guess that most mother want to care for their children so much that sometimes they give out too much information, while hoping to help them."

"Who knows?" replied Mary.

The rest of the drive was in silence as Mary kept her thoughts to herself, and for some reason he did not ask her any questions. "Is he waiting on me to say something?" Mary asked herself. She decided to keep any thoughts to herself as she marveled as his nice car, that seemed to do well in the slick roads, with some ice still left on them from the other day's snowfall.

They got to the gym, and the lady at the entrance didn't even make a sound when the doctor said that he had a friend with him that day, and he didn't get a charge. They walked up a flight of stairs to the second level of the gym and found a track that went around. The middle area of the gym was nothing more than windows looking down onto equipment and some open tennis courts. They began to walk around the track, Doctor Ross in his suit, and Mary in a pair of sweats.

"Are you worried any," he asked?

"A little bit, although there aren't that many people here. I'm glad." A few runners would lap them every couple of minutes and they passed by some equipment with a few people on each side as they walked around. Mary kept a tight eye on anyone that they passed by to see if they were watching her.

Doctor Ross caught her checking them. "Has anyone stared at you?"

"I don't think so, but I can't watch them all of the time."

"I want you to try and not think about who is watching you."

"How can I do that?"

"Would it hurt you if someone saw you and kept looking?"

"I would feel uncomfortable, but it wouldn't hurt me."

"That is a good start. Do you think that they might be staring at me since I am the only person in the building in a suit?"

"I'm sure that they noticed you," explained Mary.

"If there is just as much of a chance of people noticing me in a suit as them noticing you as a mother with loss, then when they look in this direction, remind yourself to look for the proof. Are they really staring at you, or could it be something else?"

"So what you want me to do is look for excuses not to believe what I first want to believe?"

"Yes and no. What you first believe could indeed be the truth. What we will work on is how true is it in your mind. One hundred percent true is what we want to stay away from. Anything is possible!"

"Okay," Mary answered. Many times she had no choice but to go along with the whims of the doctor. He was just so unpredictable in his requests.

"Have you spoken with your friend Pam since the accident?"

"No."

"Why not?"

"It would just seem so uncomfortable. I mean, she was there. I don't blame her, but I still second guess it, you know?"

"I know what you mean. I'm sure that you have a few long term goals for your life. Do you have any short term goals?"

"I don't know."

"Have you thought about what you want to do when you finish with your therapy?"

"I'm not sure yet. I still haven't bothered myself with it." Mary was confused on where he was going with this. Many times she could guess, but this didn't seem like his normal style, although he had a way of masking his point until it was built up well.

Hell, she wasn't even sure if she would ever even get out of therapy!

"Yes you have," he explained, but she looked confused. "You made a goal to go out and be in the public again. Today you accomplished that goal."

"Oh," she responded. "I didn't think of that as a goal."

"It is a big step one way or the other," he said. "This shows that you have more strength now than you did a few months ago. You should be proud of yourself."

"I guess. I don't feel proud. I feel the same."

"Maybe you aren't letting yourself feel good. You have told me before how you told yourself that you don't deserve happiness. Could this be a side effect of a thought like that?"

"I don't know. I guess it could be, but I didn't think about it."

"Okay, so do you think that there is a difference in your mood when comparing today to a time two months ago?"

"I guess."

"Two months ago you could scarcely leave the confinement of your room. Today you are out in the public."

"Well, yes, that is something that I wouldn't have done two months ago," she replied.

"So there is an improvement in your courage?"

"I guess. Two months ago I wouldn't have just come out here, and I wouldn't have come out here with you, when I didn't know you. Now I know you, so I guess that I can do it with you here."

"So you don't think that you could do this, if I was not here?"

"I'm sure that I couldn't do it."

"Okay, then how about we make that one of your short-term goals?"

"Okay, I guess that I can do that."

"I'm glad. You won't have to go far or with a lot of people, just a few people and for just a few minutes alone without me around."

"Okay."

"How would you feel if we give you a couple other small short-term goals?"

"I guess," she said reluctantly.

"How about a conversation with your friend Pam. It doesn't have to be long, but a conversation none the less?"

"I don't know about that one. That would be hard! There is just so much tension there between us. I don't blame her, really, but part of me is angry."

"Okay, do that after you have had a short conversation with someone not including your parents. Then you can move onto Pam when you feel a bit more comfortable and you can talk with her more relaxed about this anger that still lingers."

"I'm still not sure about this."

"You don't have to them right away. Just in time, try and do those. I'm sure that when the time is right you will have the courage and strength. When you have some interaction it doesn't even have to be someone that you know. Human interaction at any level, with people outside of your family or me at this point, will do you worlds of good."

"I'm glad that you have so much faith in me," she responded.

The two walked around another five laps or so, making a mile and a half. Mary felt a little tired, but she also felt revived as her muscles moved after so much time in her room. She hadn't walked that far in a long time, and she hadn't been that active since before her children passed. "I feel so much energy that I haven't felt lately," she said to the doctor. "Is it because I'm out moving around?"

"I'm sure that it has a big impact on your energy. With the exercise and the slightly better mood that you have been experiencing, both help energy levels. Another thing, since we are on the subject. When you exercise, a couple great mood-enhancing chemicals are pushed through your brain. So it can not only give you more energy, but make you feel better also!"

"Hm. That is interesting." Mary didn't have much to say on the subject. The doctor would always give bits of information that sooner or later would all tie into each other, but sometimes she couldn't understand it all. Maybe in time it would all come together.

The two finished one extra lap and then they proceeded back down the flight of stairs and back out into the cold. Mary was just a little warm from her walk, so the cold air did not effect her as much as it would have. The drive back was not any more talkative than the drive to the gym, but Mary seemed like a slightly different person. She looked out of her window into the gray sky and noticed the clouds move here and there, and she reminded herself that she wanted to feel happiness again sooner or later down the line. And although it was still strange to smile, she let out a smile just to feel the muscles in her face move again. The drive went by quickly and Mary was back home. Doctor Ross walked her to her door and just before she walked in he touched her arm and said, "Remember, Mary-today was an accomplishment. Think of it that way." With that he turned around and headed back to his car, and Mary walked inside her home and looked around to see that her mother was not waiting for her, so she proceeded quickly as not to be noticed, to her room to reflect on her thoughts.

Evening came soon and Mary was almost looking forward to her parents asking about her walk with the doctor. She knew that she didn't want them to drill her, but like a mixed feeling college kid home for Christmas she wanted to talk with them regardless. Mary walked downstairs when dinner was ready and found her place at the table. She didn't want to seem too enthusiastic, as she still didn't want to give them an impression that she was "healed" or anything of the sort. They began to eat, and her mother couldn't hold back her curiosity any longer.

"How was the walk with Doctor Ross?"

"It was okay, I guess," responded Mary subtly.

"How do you like him as a doctor, Mary?" her father asked.

"I think that he is good. He is very controlled, but he can also be funny every now and then."

"He is cute too!"

"Mom! He is married!"

"So, he is still cute. No harm in looking."

"He's my doctor! Okay, no more about this subject." As Mary said that she was not only frustrated that her mother was so nosy about her life, but she also felt somewhat exhilarated at the fight. Although it was not a yelling fight, more of a playful argument, it made Mary feel like a person again. "Could even negative interaction help my illness?"

"It does seem strange though, that he would give so much special treatment," inquired her father.

"He wanted me to go to a Saturday group thing that he does with some of his patients, but I didn't want to, so he took me to the gym. I don't know. He seems to hint that he goes out of his way with some patients to help them individually."

"Well, he seemed convinced of his methods from the first day, so who knows? I'm sure that it will work out fine in the end."

The next day found Mary in a mood of self-actualization and hope. For the first time in months Mary was able to see some light at the end of the tunnel. Although every time that she would seem to hope for something more, she could feel negative feelings holding her back, she did her best to push forward. She was determined to use her will power to overcome her adversities, but it still seemed so hard, and though she could feel more hope, it would quickly fade and she would have to fight for it back again. Life would not hold her down forever and like a slow moving snail with a distance seemingly unreachable, but it could be captured in time.

Mary fought with her hope and doubts every day leading up to her next appointment with the doctor. She made many entries into her notebook, both of her sad times, and now of her hopeful times, but one thing still dwelled on her mind. She wanted to do one of her "short-term" goals before she would see the doctor again. She wanted to show him that she could do the hard work if he counted on her, and since he believed so greatly in her, she would do her best not to let him down. She thought and thought of how she could accomplish one of those hard tasks before Wednesday, then finally it hit her, "The mailman," she yelled to herself. "He has to walk in the snow, and if it is cold outside he won't want to spend any time at all in a conversation. I can just say hi, he will say hi, and that will be it!" It was Monday night when her thought occurred so she could not wait until the next day to catch him as he came by. "But how am I going to go out there, just for kicks, in the cold? I'll go out to pick up the mail, like it was already delivered, and I'll act surprised to see him! Yes, that is what I'll do. Do you think that he will realize what was happening?"

The next day came, and she waited near a window downstairs, so that she could peer out into the street. With all of the days inside that she spent, it made her ponder why she hadn't realized the time of the mailman after spending the last two months or so inside. She shuddered off the thought and resumed her vigil self, while peering out the window. She waited and almost fell asleep as boredom moved through her mind in waves, becoming stronger each time. Then, just before two in the afternoon, she could see him walking briskly up the street. A few houses down the man was spotted, and Mary jumped up and grabbed her coat. She threw it on quickly and walked back to the window to see how far away he was. She would have to walk out as he was next door. "Can I do this? Maybe I shouldn't do this; it seems so strange. Okay, I'm not going to do this. No! I must; I can do this. I can do this. I *will* do this." Mary got back up and waited for the mailman. Finally he came to the next door and Mary rushed to her door and walked outside like she had no idea what was happening. She felt nervous, her fingers were shaking and she wasn't even sure if she could speak as she walked down the path to the box.

She acted as though it was a total surprise to see him as she came to the box. He came closer. He was almost there. "Can I do this? Yes! Oh God."

"Hello," she forced out, but the quiver was quite noticeable, although the man could have no other thought than to blame the freezing weather.

"Hi," he answered with a slight chatter of his teeth. He came closer and as he did he put the mail out in front of him and handed it to her as he came by.

"Stay warm," she sounded as he handed her the pile of junk mail.

"I'm working on it. Have a good day."

"You too," Mary mumbled out. Her lips were shaking, she could hardly talk, but it was not only because of the cold. She had pushed so much adrenaline to talk to him that she was shaking all over her body. Her fingers and lips shook more as she walked to the front door. Before it was just nervousness, but in the act of accomplishing her goal her body was jump-started with energy and her shakes came as the result. "I did it. I did it! Hell, I could have talked longer." Mary did not know if she was feeling better and that helped her that day, or that she had hardly talked to anyone in so long that she just needed to let out so many words. It was like friends who hadn't seen each other in years, trying to exchange one thousand stories in just moments. Mary gave herself a small smile, happy with her accomplishment, and maybe more happy to know that she could brag to the doctor the following day. Indeed vanity may be the world's strongest push for accomplishment.

Mary felt accomplishment, true accomplishment, for the first time in ages, it seemed. She just paced her room at the end of her day, much like her normal pacing, but instead of forcing together thoughts and pacing with an angry and disgruntled look painted on her face, she seemed to move with an air of confidence. With so much unbridled enthusiasm for her work she could not help but pat herself on the back time after time. Mary could not sleep without thinking deep thoughts about the implications of it all, and what the doctor would then want out of her. She still had a couple goals to accomplish, but she felt more than a step closer, even if the road was still thousands of steps long. Mary paced and wondered what her life was like. She could see so many negative things, that it was harder and harder for her to remember her accomplishment as she measured it to past failures. It was like her mind was playing a mean game on her: one minute she was confident and happy, and the next she was moments away from tears. She paced and debated each thought in her mind for hours before she could go to sleep. But after one in the morning, Mary decided that sleep would be important if she was to battle her own mind again the next day. Mary rested her head on her pillow, and allowed the soft and cozy feeling to just sink in. She rested her mind so that she could sleep, and it did not take long for it to come.

The next morning came, and after some time, Mary found herself in a daze, doing nothing more than gently tossing her pillow into the air and then catching it. The action was that of a youthful person, and although she was still young she was not that young. Mary thought for another moment being too old to play, but then let the thought fall away and allowed herself to enjoy the simplicity of the harmonic motions. Her mind idled along thinking about the day to come, and without any feeling of ambition to do another one of her goals that day, she just tossed the pillow a few inches into the air and then grabbed hold of it again on its descent. Her mind traveled from reminding herself that she was going to ask the doctor about her ever-changing mood, and how she debated how she would spend her day until that time came. In the meantime the pillow found its way up again, and then down again, like a pendulum of a clock. The motion seemed to become harmonic as she spent just the same amount of time with the pillow in her hands, and in the air, each throw. Her mind dwelled more on her erratic sleeping patterns, as well. She couldn't discern why she would sleep for so many hours for a number of days in a row and then turn around and not be able to fall asleep for another few days. Her insomnia and hypersomnia confused her, but she tossed the pillow without a break in the motion.

Mary continued through her daze for fifteen minutes without a break. She did not think of it as pointless, boring, or saddening, but she was indifferent to it on all fronts. Her body and mind had seemed to be on sleep mode as she felt no emotion at all, and seemed to reject any emotions at the thoughts she was having. It seemed so strange, but at the same time, so refreshing to release her mind from its constant struggle, like a weary warrior taking a breath in the middle of battle to regroup himself. And for that fifteen minutes Mary's mind was able to take that deep breath in its battle and allow itself time away from thoughts, whether they possessed positive or negative qualities.

Before long, though, the battle found its way back into her psyche and she tossed down her pillow and went downstairs to help herself to breakfast, with a mind full of thoughts and emotions. She ate her breakfast as her mother tried to make small talk with her, but since her life hadn't changed in so long, it almost seemed pointless. Her mother would have loved to speak about her progress with the doctor, but any time that the conversation began to drift in that manner, Mary would let out quick, "I don't really feel like talking about it," and her mother would ease off. Mary could feel that she was getting better. Or was it just a phantom? She was still afraid not to get her parents' hopes up. She felt her mind as an overburdened bridge, and although the load was slowly being lifted, she still feared its collapse.

Mary finished her meal and went to her room to write in her notebook. He hadn't said much about her first notebook, and she wondered what he would think of this second. She tried to let the thought go and began to write about what she felt, her day, how she dazed off, and every thought that followed in her mind as she wrote, and just as importantly she reminded herself to make a considerable entry for yesterday's work. She began to feel that her writing was an outlet for her emotions. Mary laughed at herself. She could feel laughter more easily then, and although her mind still dwelled on her children, she could feel her life trying to move on. But, just as before, when she found herself smiling or laughing, or even feeling better than normal, her mind would quickly shift to more depressing thoughts. At some point her mind would even tell herself that she couldn't be happy again, and that her happiness was not a prelude to a better life, but a momentary glitch in her life as it was then. She wrote more in her book about it, and then wrote it on her hand. "Why do I shift from happy thoughts and almost a gleeful disposition into a melancholy mood?"

She looked at her hand for a moment seeing the black ink as it traced itself throughout her tiny wrinkles in the skin, and was hit by another thought. "And why does it shift so quickly?" She underlined the second question, as it plagued her more than the former. She had the feeling that he would say her own thoughts made for some chemical problem, but she could not imagine what he would say about the brevity of her joy. The time then passed quickly; as she ate lunch and waited for her father. He had taken Wednesday afternoon off each week since her therapy started to take her to and from therapy. It also gave him a chance to be with her, and maybe get some insight into her depression, but of course he would never say that.

She waited, minutes before he was scheduled to be home, staring out aimlessly through her window, gazing at her tree. Mary did not know where her life was going from there. It seemed like she was still fighting day to day, and she tried not to think of the future yet. Besides she still had two more goals to accomplish, "Oh," she cried to herself, as her father drove up to the house. "I need to write it down, or I will forget." She rushed over to a pen and wrote on her hand that she had accomplished one of her goals, almost as if she would forget it. Mary wondered aimlessly sometimes constantly questioning if she did something or if she would remember a thought. It almost seemed as though even the most mundane of tasks brought forth a fear that she would somehow forget what she was doing and leave it undone. Mary lost the thought as she looked forward to the session ahead. The objectivity she once had of determining the doctor's worth was drifting away, as he seemed to be more of a credible source for knowledge as the weeks passed. She smiled for just a moment, grabbed her coat, and headed down the stairs to greet her father.

Before she blinked she was in Doctor Ross' office being greeted by his smile and good nature. There was almost something borderline unprofessional about his ever-cheerful ways. She thought that maybe it was a facade he would put on for his patients, or maybe it was his own advice in action. Maybe he spent his time controlling his thoughts and emotions and what not.

"Hello Mary, how are you today," he said while motioning for her to take a seat.

"Okay, I guess," she responded as he found his normal seat.

"How was your week?"

"I'm glad that you asked," she responded cheerfully. "I attained one of my goals!"

"That is excellent," he responded. "Tell me about it."

"Well, I wanted to just make a simple conversation, and I didn't think that I could do that with Pam yet, but I talked to the postman."

"That is good. How long did you spend with him?" asked the doctor.

"No long," said Mary, frowning a bit.

"Don't worry if it wasn't a long time," reassured Ross. "Every little bit counts. Please go on."

"There isn't much else, but I met him out as he came by with the mail. We just said hi, and I told him to stay warm, and then have a good day. Not much."

"But that is good Mary. I'm proud of you, that was a tough step, but you did it. Tell me though, was there any point when you felt as though you would not be able to go through with it?"

"Yes, right before I went out, on my way out, hours before I went out, and just about every second in between."

"What did you tell yourself that made you go out there?"

"I'm not sure. I think I just reassured myself that I *could* do it, and that I was strong enough."

"That is excellent," replied Ross with a more than pleased tone. He leaned across his desk and gave her a yellow notepad. "I want you to write that down three times," he said.

"What?"

"I want you to write, 'I can do anything that I set my mind to' three times on that pad please."

"Okay," she complied. She wrote it three times, but even as the pen passed over the yellow paper she had conflicting thoughts of the doctor's own mental health, but just as she finished she reminded herself that all of his strange ways haven't been too wrong so far.

"Good. Now write it three times again, and each time that you write it, think about the tough task that you accomplished and remember how you faced up to what was hard."

"Okay." She wrote it three more times.

He took the pad from her. "Excellent. Anything else exciting happen to you during your week?"

"I have a question for you," she responded almost trying to stay away from the question.

"Okay."

"I have been finding myself in a good mood sometimes, mostly when I think that I have accomplished something, or I think that I might be on the right road to feeling better, or something like that. And then I start to feel bad, like I can't reach that goal, and I remember all of the tough things that brought me to where I am. And it happens so fast!"

"Do you believe that you can be happy again?" he asked.

"Yes," she said, tilting her head down just a bit.

"Are you sure?" he questioned again. "You can be happier. You will be happier. You will be happy again."

"I know," she said again, somewhat uncomfortable with what he was saying. She moved her head quickly and looked at the floor, trying not to make eye contact with him.

"Are you sure that you know?" he asked. "You can be happy again. You will be."

"I know," she said again, still unable to look at his eyes. Even though she had been through so much already, Mary's mind still held on to some of her guilt. Why was that? She could not tell you, but the guilt was still lingering behind. He was trying too hard to uncover it.

Doctor Ross leaned forward and with a slightly lighter voice. "You can be. You are stronger than you think, and you will be happy again."

"Okay, I know. Why do you keep telling me that?"

"I know that it is tough to believe it. Do you remember a while back when I asked you if you could believe that you would be happy again, and you said that you didn't know? I'm asking you now to tell me what you believe. I need a yes or no, Mary."

"I-I-I."

"You can be. You will be," he interrupted as she let out a few tears, her mind overwhelmed with thoughts. She almost felt as if she had left the room and her mind was once again in a strange state of being.

"It just seems so hard. Why are you doing this to me?"

"When you see yourself happy, don't let pessimism stop you from believing. It will happen more times in the future. You will see light, and think that dark will overcome it, you must believe that you can be happy, and that you deserve happiness." Mary began to cry harder. "You have the strength. You can do anything that you want. You can be happy."

"I-I." Still sobbing. "It is just so hard to believe! It doesn't seem true."

"Believe it, Mary," he said again. "You can, and if you ever doubt it, remember that you could go out there to meet that postman. You did have the strength, and you will have the strength again. And your strength will grow; it will multiply, and every time that you gather your courage you will find more of it."

Mary cried more and more, her mind trying to overcome the implanted thoughts that she was not strong enough, and breaking down in emotions trying to believe. "And no matter what, Mary," he said again. "No matter how strong you are or how weak you might be sometimes, don't ever forget that you never have to do it on your own. I will always be here if you need, and so will your parents. You are a strong person, but everyone needs a shoulder. If you ever need that shoulder, they are around, but don't doubt yourself. You are strong, and you will be happy. I am confident of that."

Mary cried for a few more minutes and Doctor Ross remained silent with a box of tissue in his hands. He allowed her to gain composure once more. "This is the last big step Mary," he started. "After this it is all downhill. Don't let anyone ever tell you that you don't deserve happiness, and never tell yourself that. If you can do those two things then all of this pain and suffering will soon go away."

Mary was still overwhelmed.

"I want to believe. I don't deserve happiness if my family is gone. What kind of mother would I be? They would want you to be happy! Don't be afraid of being happy."

"But I am! If I become happy again, what will it do to their memory? It will be lost."

"No! If I do nothing for me then all of our memories are lost, and I'll just be here suffering. I can do this. God I hope so."

"Mary, do you mind if I take your latest notebook home with me so that I can read it?" he began again as she stopped her crying.

"No, go ahead," she replied still surprised at the quick change of subject.

"Excellent, and I have another one for you," he said.

"How many of these do I have to do?"

"This is your last one, and it is just for you." She looked at him puzzled. "Mary, in this notebook I want you to put down what thoughts bring you to tears, and what thinking that you should do in that situation to solve the problem."

"I'm not sure that I know what you mean," she questioned.

"I think you do." She still looked puzzled. "Whenever we talk about the thoughts that make you think negatively, they are always thoughts that you produce. If you don't want them to take over you like that, you must realize what you are thinking, the moment that it happens, and reassure yourself that some of them may be frivolous."

"I am still lost."

"Say you were to think of a happy thought and then you think of the trouble that you have faced. At instances like that, you cannot allow yourself to think that you will never be happy again, because you know that it isn't true. In this notebook, it is up to you to remind yourself of how you are stronger than you will think sometimes. This notebook will be for you and you alone. I will never need to read it, because as you write down what happened, and how you think it could have been prevented, and after all of that, you remind yourself that you are strong, and that you deserve happiness. After it is all said and done you won't need me anymore."

"So what you are saying is that once I get to the point where I can realize my negative thoughts and correct them, I won't ever need you again?"

"That is correct. Of course, it never hurts to seek therapy, but you will be able to help yourself, and keep yourself in check. Therapy will become nothing more than a check-up like a doctor's visit. Of course you will still face hardship, but as you start really focusing on your thoughts, the hard times will pass quickly and, in the case of your emotions, quietly."

"So this is like what you told me about a few weeks ago. That after I solve this, everything will seem easier and better?"

"Exactly. You should still come for a few more sessions, but soon it will all start coming together, much sooner than you think."

Mary thought about that for the rest of the session. She had just been through tears and trying to reassure herself that she would find happiness, and he had the guts to tell her that it would come sooner than she realized. How could he always be so optimistic? Mary went on her way when the time came, carrying her new notebook with her, and as she walked out into the world, she seemed to breathe different air. It no longer contained the stench of black hazy clouds without any rays of hope or light to penetrate them. She stared up at the clear blue sky, with the few clouds moving slowly through the sky, and into the bright yellow sun. She ignored the cold as she drew in breath after breath of clean air that made her lungs beg for more. She felt like a prisoner let free after years of solitude and confinement. She felt as though her life would be beginning again from that point, like the past no longer controlled her, and that it could not hold her back from her life. Mary did not feel confident enough to spring back into life as a normal person, but in the brief ten seconds that it took her to walk out to the car, her mind moved faster than ever. She would call her friend Pam, and have her over for dinner, and she would talk with her, and let her anger go. Mary was still angry with her for the entire situation, and she would rectify the situation and bring closure to that problem of her life, and in doing so, she would also attain the feeling of accomplishment from capturing yet another goal. Maybe she could be happy. Hell, stranger things had happened. Mary smiled as the ride home took her to a new state of life; one that she had been missing for so long. Though try as she might she knew that sooner or later that night, before she retired for bed, she would have to go over her revelations in therapy. Mary wasn't looking forward to the hours of time it might take her to organize all of her thoughts so she concentrated on her knew goal at hand.

As soon as she got home and as fast as she could get the phone before the nerve left her, she called her friend Pam. Her hands shook as she dialed the number, and her lips shook, and her throat was tight as she heard her friend answer the phone. She was relieved that her husband did not answer the phone and give her more conversation than she needed.

"Hello," came the friendly voice.

"Hello Pam, this is Mary," she said in a quick and monotone thrust.

"Oh, hello Mary. How are you doing?" responded Pam in a soft voice.

"I'm doing okay. I was hoping that you would like to have lunch tomorrow."

"I would love to. What do you have in mind?" Pam said surprised.

"Would you mind coming over here, and we can just have whatever?" asked Mary, still shaking and quick with her words.

"That would be great. I'll come over near eleven thirty or so."

"Okay, Pam. I would like to talk longer, but I'm sure that we will have a chance tomorrow. I'll see you then."

"Sounds good, bye."

"Bye," sounded Mary. Her lips were still shaking and her mind was nearly blown away. She hardly believed that could happen, and she was glad that she decided to call while she was still on her high from the therapy session. She was glad that she would have another goal accomplished, but what would she say? Did she have the strength to actually go through with this? "Yes," she thought. "I can do this. I am strong enough. I have a new lease on life; I have to hit it hard! But it will be so hard. I know, but I can do this. Remember what the doctor said, I can't forget it. I am stronger than I think. We will be able to give up these feelings that are bottled up about Pam, we can talk with her. Pam will understand; she is nice. But what if she isn't? What if she gets defensive and I get angry and we fight? No! I'm sure that everything will work out. Will it? Oh, God."

Mary argued with herself for just a few moments longer, but decided that she could deal with Pam, it was only lunch anyway, and she wouldn't stay very long. Mary reminded herself of her previous difficulties, of talking to the postman and of going to the gym around other people, and with that on her mind, she continued to tell herself that she would be fine. But, this was no two-line conversation that she would soon have. This was going to be a discussion with the woman behind the wheel when her children were killed.

The rest of the evening came and went, and Mary soon found herself preparing for sleep. She put her nightgown on and lifted her lock-it to see the pictures inside. She stood, slightly cold with the air being chilled through the window, and her thin layer of clothing doing little to stop it. But the cold did not bother her as she stood, and once more she found herself beside time, remembering good times with her family as her eyes could not leave their faces. She remembered the sad times as well, and felt their loss in her heart. She knew that it would be fine to cry over them at that time, but she had cried so much that day already that she just felt the pain in her heart and left it at that. Through the dark cloud in her heart, a small breeze made its way through the labyrinth of her heart. She knew that she would never find a replacement for them, and that she would probably never try, and she knew that she would always feel pain from them, but she felt as though, they had finally allowed her to think about something else; to be selfish for once. She knew that she had never told the doctor, and she wasn't sure if she would, due to fear of him thinking her crazy, but she felt obligated to them to feel sad. He was right though, she had not allowed herself to believe that she deserved happiness, or could even accomplish it, but what plagued her more was that she did not believe her family would want her to lose her depression. But with the realization of the evening, she peered at the pictures and allowed herself to forget the idea that they wanted her to feel bad. "They would want me to be happy," she thought to herself. "We all loved each other so much." Mary became teary eyed, but she breathed in deep and relaxed at the thought of happy times. She had made so many revelations that day; her mind and body could be nothing but tired. She held tight her family in her hand and told herself that if she felt worried about tomorrow with her friend, that they would be there for her, just as she had also wanted to be there for them. She smiled to herself, allowed the platinum heart to fall to her own, and she moved herself into her bed. Mary rested her head on her pillow, felt the feathers, as it was a true feather pillow, and let her mind move away from the scene and to one of pleasure and fantasy. She saw herself on a beach sometime far from there, holding her children in her arms, with her loving husband putting his hand on her cheek and smiling as he moved his thumb over her ear, and conveying all his love with his constant eye contact. She knew that with her final thoughts of the day all would be all right in her life sometime down the road. Mary did not think much longer and her mind went to sleep wishing that someday, maybe in Heaven, that scene would be her soul's everlasting resting place. There was a momentary joy that Mary could feel coming into her life. For the first time in as long as she could remember, she pictured heaven as something wonderful. She had seen her life in such Hell, and her self-esteem had forced her to believe that when she died, Hell would await her. It was odd to her as the thought passed and she slipped away, but she could feel it deep in her mind, and that was enough to burden her and she could stay awake no longer.

The next day found its way, and Mary's awakening interrupted her dreaming. She did not remember much of it as she crawled out of bed. "Something about whales and a boat. That is so weird. Let's not try and find meaning in that," she thought to herself as she moved into the bathroom for her shower. She did not anticipate her meeting with her friend, and in truth she feared it a bit, but she grabbed her platinum heart, and closed her eyes, as water trickled down her face, and remembered that she was not alone in her endeavors.

The time passed and Mary soon found her friend knocking on the door. Mary swallowed the lump in her throat, and tried to force the shaking of her hands to stop, but unable, she accepted it and opened the door.

"Hello Pam," she started as she saw her friend's emotionless face. It looked as though no expression had founds its home there in months. "Please come in," Mary started trying to hide her shake.

Pam moved in and Mary motioned for her to follow her to the dinning table, just a few feet away from the door. "I made a few sandwiches. I hope you like tuna fish."

"Yes, I do," replied Pam. "How have you been?"

"Not too great, but I'm feeling a little better now," began Mary, feeling very nervous still, but dealing with it the best that she could.

"I haven't had a chance to tell you Mary, but I am so sorry for this. I have felt so guilty, and it has been tearing me apart."

"No, don't feel guilty Pam. It was the truck's fault. I do not hold you responsible," consoled Mary. The words almost seemed wrong though; Mary wasn't still sure whom to blame. With the apology from her friend, Mary was beginning to warm up slightly to the conversation, but she still wanted to keep her distance. "Pam, one of the reasons for inviting you over here, was for me to apologize to you." Pam's face turned to a confused look. "You see, I blamed you for a while, and then I blamed myself. But I was very angry with you, and although you never heard it from me, I felt, well to be honest, infuriated with you. I wanted to apologize to you, not only because I don't feel that way now, but also I never had the right to be angry with you, and although I never said anything to you, I needed to say sorry, for the thoughts that I had. Do you know what I mean?"

"Yes. I'm so glad that you called me," replied Pam. "I just want you to know how bad I have been feeling."

Moments later, after a brief silence, Mary headed to the kitchen to get the sandwiches. She had put out some chips already, but no drinks. "What can I get you to drink, Pam?"

"A Diet Coke, if you have it." Mary came back with the sandwiches and two Diet Cokes. They sat down and began to eat.

"I'm sure that it has been really tough Mary, and if you don't want to talk about any of this, then, I won't ask any questions."

"It is okay, Pam. I might break down, but I'll tell you if we need to change the subject," replied Mary. "I haven't been out much, but I have gone to see that Doctor Ross for that last two months or so."

"Oh, how is he? Is he good?"

"He is really good. I think he is the only therapist in town that doesn't give out prescriptions."

"After the children," started Pam. "I went to Doctor Wilson because I was feeling so guilty, and he gave me some pills that make me feel a little better. He is nice though."

"I tell you though, my guy seems so strange," said Mary, feeling a little better that they were talking about someone else beyond her, and it was refreshing to know that she wasn't the only one in therapy. "I have to analyze my thoughts all the time. I also have to write in this notebook, and he doesn't believe in pills at all. But he has made me feel a little better. I am making progress, so I can't complain about that." Mary thought to herself on what she had just said. "Was that the first time that I believed he was really doing her some good?"

"Well that is great," replied Pam smiling. "Do you plan on staying in town, or do you think that you will go back to St. Paul?"

"I don't know yet. I'm still kind of in limbo. I still have a lot more mourning to do, and I'm not sure that I could even feel up to a work place right now."

"Well that is okay, Mary. If I was in your place I would take at least a year off and just try to rebuild a little bit. Not many people go through what you have in the last three years."

"I'm glad that you said that," responded Mary. The rest of the conversation seemed to go by quickly as the two talked about old times a little bit, and some about their therapists. Mary tried her best not to allow the conversation to make its way back to her children so that she would not cry with her friend there. After about one, Pam said that she needed to get back, and although part of Mary wanted more time, most of her was glad to get back to her solitude. Mary felt that she had accomplished a lot more today than just a simple short-term goal. She was finally getting back to the real world and talking with real people again. She had grown fond of her alone time though, and was happy to not have to spend very long with her friend. Mary's guard was still up. She enjoyed the company, yes, but

Mary was never sure how much she would be able to take before her barrier of her wailing emotions would burst, and she didn't want anyone to see her when she did. Mary went up to her room to rest and relax, and to write in her "journal." Since the doctor was not going to look at this new notebook, Mary decided to deem it a journal of her life from that moment on. "I'll put down every major thought, every major event, and maybe even day to day nonsense in it," she thought to herself. "That is what a journal is for, right? Maybe if I treat it like that, then it will really help me." She began to write and did not stop for an hour. She put most of her conversation with Pam onto the paper and her thoughts on everything. She smiled as she finished and paced a bit, thinking of everything that had happened as she waited, anxiously, for dinner.

The net few days passed without many breakdowns, and Mary was determined to not allow herself thoughts that were without reason or logic. "They do nothing but hurt me." She spent nearly two hours a day writing in her notebook about her thoughts, her feelings, and every now and then she was able to put in a hope or two. For Mary the time was finally passing a bit more smoothly, and although her sleeping was still erratic, her nights were becoming more congruent with each night previous to it.

The day came, next Wednesday, and for the first time since her therapy had started, Mary was excited about seeing the doctor and helping herself. She wanted to tell him about her latest accomplishment, and how she was controlling her thoughts, and not allowing herself to become overwhelmed too easily. Doctor Ross taught her to "look for the proof," and she was trying to practice that everyday. She began to write even more furiously in her journal, and wanted him to see her writing also, even if he didn't need to. Mary was becoming proud of her diligence of work once again. She hadn't had that feeling since high school, and it felt good to show off just a bit.

The afternoon came and Mary walked into the doctor's office to see him smiling as he always did.

"Hello Mary. Please take a seat. How are you today?"

"I'm pretty good, actually."

"Today is a landmark day," he began again. "Today you came in and told me that your day was good. Pretty good at that! I'm so glad to hear it, and I would love for you to tell me why."

"Well, I talked with my friend Pam last Thursday!"

"That is terrific. What did you two talk about?"

"Everything, I guess. She came over and we had lunch. I told her that I was sorry for holding her accountable for a while, even though I never told her or you for that matter. And she apologized, she felt guilty about it all. We talked about you, and her shrink, I don't know."

"That is good," explained the doctor nodding his head. "How did that make you feel?"

"Well, at first I was a nervous wreck, and even during the whole thing, I had my guard up and I felt a little shake in my hands, but at the end of it all, I felt good to have done it."

"Feel good because you got the apology off or your chest, or because you accomplished another goal?"

"Both."

"That is great, Mary. I'm proud of you."

"You know, there is something else on my mind that has been forming lately, but it seems so strange, I'm not sure how I can even say it."

"Well, just do your best," he answered.

"I have been feeling strangely. I know that I am still depressed, and that I still have some work to go before I can get myself to work with others again and get back into daily life with the rest of humanity, but I feel so liberated. I feel like the path that would take be back to that life was a long road and I had to walk on my feet. But lately since I have been feeling so much better, it is like I'm in a car, driving faster and faster every good thought that I have, and every time that I am able to control my emotions. I've been trying to look out for my automatic thoughts, like you told me to, and I think I'm doing okay on them too."

"That is good, Mary."

"I don't know what it is, but since last week, you have opened my eyes, and I finally believe, I truly believe that I can be happy again."

"I'm glad for you Mary, but it was not my doing. I only point the way, you decided to work for it. It is your courage and commitment that has gotten you this far."

"I'm not sure about that. You have helped me, and I can't believe you would after I hit you so hard a few months back. I never would have thought that I could confront my friend about my children."

"And as great as those accomplishments are, just as you mentioned earlier we have a couple more steps to go, but these will not be as hard as any of the former. And the most important aspect that you are missing is that you can never forget that you have the control over your life. No matter what happens in your life, always remember that life has less to do with your experiences and more to do with how you react to them. But as for now, we have to work on the next step."

"So what do you have in mind? I know that you want me to go to a larger group, and I think that I'm going to go to church with my family on Sunday."

"That is great, Mary. I have been reading over your notebook from the last few weeks. I must say that I am quite impressed by the sheer volume of writing that is in this," he said as he raised the notebook from his desk. Mary didn't say anything. "I am glad that you decided to put in, not only thoughts that led up to your breakdowns, but other thoughts as well."

"I'm impressed that you could read any of it, because my mind wandered so much while writing it."

"Oh, that is the best part," explained Ross. "It gives me a view of your mind as you see it-not as an edited, abridged copy. I get a look at the real thing. He was happy to see that Mary joined him in the laugh, even if it was only momentary. "Tell me, Mary. Do you have an idea of what you want to do when you go out for another job?"

"No, I haven't really thought about it," she returned.

"That is okay, but this week, especially when your thoughts are dwelling on your church visit, I want you to also think about what you plan to do when you get to the end of that road."

"Okay," she responded. "I think that I can handle that. Oh, I want you to see something more." She pulled out her journal from her bag that she carried with her. She handed him the notebook saying, "I have been writing even more in this one, and I know that you said that you didn't need to see it, I wanted you to anyway. I have been writing for like two hours each day."

"Wow, Mary." He poured over the writing as quickly as he could, trying not to waste time, but still spend enough to not make her feel as though he did not care. "Ah, I see you're writing about what you were just talking about," he said as he read through one of the pages. "I don't want you to go without this, Mary," he said as he handed it back to her. "I need to finish going over this other one first, but if you would like to put another week's worth of writing into it, I would love to read it more thoroughly next week, if you would allow me?"

"I would like that," replied Mary, but somewhat offended that he did not take it. At first she did not want to believe that he was being realistic, but she tried to remember that he had done so much for her up until that point, and it would be useless to give up now. Besides it wouldn't be in his character to try and hurt her feelings. "Good, that's good. Try to hold those thoughts." She liked that idea that her work made him want to read over it more carefully. That couldn't mean that he thought she might be crazy with all of her strange writing. Could it? Mary shrugged off those thoughts as she was reminded, again, of how much she trusted him now. He had been nice and optimistic for so long, she couldn't see him as untrustworthy.

The rest of the session went by, in Mary's mind, quickly. She seemed to have lost herself for a while though, pondering thoughts and pouring over her examination of his office, and although he could notice her inattention, Doctor Ross took it well and in stride. He made a point not to reprimand, and he could only see it as more of her energy and mind coming back into reality. It surprised her that she hadn't spent so much time with it up until that moment, but today she made up for lost time as she noticed a couple of paintings on his wall, a diploma, and lots of books. But the session did end, and she went on her way feeling much of the same feelings that she had just a week before. A lingering thought in the back of her mind was telling her that perhaps her lack of attention was a sign of growth on her behalf, and maybe her necessity of a therapist would soon come to an end. Although she dismissed the thought thinking of how it couldn't hurt and she was sure it would help to continue, it made a sleek smile come to her face as the very thought made her feel like she was back in the "real world."

Mary promised herself over and over that she would go to church on Sunday, trying desperately not to give her mind a chance to talk her out of it. She still didn't want to tell her parents, though telling them would make it harder not to go as she tried to protect them from lost hope, but she still didn't want that pressure on herself. Mary figured that if she could not talk herself into going to church and socializing for a while, then it wouldn't be good for her to force it. Mary was happy with that thought to herself as her day ended as it normally had, resting her head on her soft pillow contemplating her life.

"He wanted me to think about where my life is going to go after all of this," she whispered to herself with her lips slightly slowed as they partly rested on the pillow. "I don't know what I will do. Is that okay? Should I know what I'm going to do already? Maybe he is trying to push me forward, because I have been moving slowly. Could that be it? No! I doubt he would be that manipulative. So far he has been telling me about all of the treatment as we did it, why would he not tell the whole truth now? I'm tired. But how can I sleep when I have such an important topic on my mind. I'll think about it tomorrow. No! What justice would I make for myself if I didn't put importance on this? Can I go back to work at a restaurant? Should I go to school? Why is this so difficult? Maybe I should wait." Mary looked at her wall and watched a small, barely noticeable, shadow move on it and then move back and forth. It was the shadow of a tree branch. "Moonlight. Hmm. I don't know where I'm to go from here, but I do need my sleep. I'll work with this tomorrow, I promise. I'm tired." Her mind fell away and sleep came upon her as the pressuring and overwhelming importance of her future rest on her shoulders, and sadly it would not leave anytime soon as the next day, and thus her waking, would bring it all back.

The days passed and before she knew it, Sunday morning found its way to her bed as she looked at the clock and heard it buzz the moment eight o'clock found its way. "I could just close my eyes, and I wouldn't have to go," she thought to herself. "It would be so easy. No! I can do this. But why? It would be so easy just to do it next week, and it would be so simple just to sleep now. No! I don't want to go back to Doctor Ross and tell him that I talked myself out of this, and I don't want that feeling. Let's get up." With that she forced herself to sit up, making it ten times as difficult to go to sleep again. She dragged herself to the shower, and smiled at the idea that this would bring a surprise to her parents. Oddly enough the warm water had become soothing again. She worried about her morning to come, but to ease her suffering she held tight her platinum heart and remembered all of the tools that she now had to defend her emotions. Her shower went by and she kept her mind on the surprise. Her parents would be excited just to see her up at that early in the morning, but she would soon walk down there dressed up and ready to go. Hopefully they would not come up and invite her before she had the chance to astonish them.

She lucked out, and she was able to change into a black dress before they came upstairs, as they had every other Sunday for the last four months. Mary put on her shoes and walked down the stairs. Her parents were busy, walking to the kitchen or their bedroom or the living room, but both stopped dead in their tracks as she walked slowly down the stairs. And like a princess on her way to a ball, she stood upright, and they, as if they were admiring a princess, fell short on words and just watched every movement as she walked, praying that her image reflected the thought they wished her to have.

"I would like to go to church with you today," proclaimed Mary.

"O-O-Okay," gasped her mother. "We will be ready in a few minutes."

Mary sat down at the dinner table and waited for them as she argued with her mind on whether or not she could actually go through with this. "Too late now!" Her dread of a lot of people watching her or even staring seemed more plausible at a place where greeting and talking to each other was much more common than any gym. She worried about how she could handle it, and then she worried more about the doctor not being there, but then again she told herself that it was all in her mind. The tide of strength moved back and forth, for what seemed like a thousand times, in the fifteen minutes that she waited for her parents to get ready. But one way or the other, she knew that there was no turning back now. She was obligated to go, and she would go.

She was nervous as they sat in the car on their way. Luckily they were going to the early service, and there would be considerably less people there. Mary smiled to her self for just a second remembering that she was doing something hard, and the fact that she was in the car at that moment showed more courage than she had for a while. Her heart raced and her hands sweat as she stepped out of the car. She could feel the sun on her face, and the cold air conflicting with it as they both tangled themselves on her skin. The air felt threatening though, but as Mary's father put his arm around her, she felt slightly better. He would help her, if she started to cry, "But I won't cry," she said to herself. "I can be strong. I will be strong. I am stronger than I ever thought that I could be. And at the least, I'm at a church, so maybe all I will have to do is pray." She swallowed the lump that made a home in her throat for the morning and walked into the foyer.

She was greeted with a smile from a man, and he didn't seem to stare or make any looks. "Good. One down, and only fifty to go." Mary tried to breathe deep as they walked down the aisle and found a pew. She noticed a few glances by people, but she reminded herself what the doctor had told her. "It might just be a coincident. Don't take offense at a look. Just relax and you will be fine," she said to herself three times as quickly as she could. Mary tried to look at the back of the pew in front of her, but to her bad luck a friend of her parent's came over to greet them. "Remember, you control your emotions, not them!"

After a moment of speaking with her mother, the old lady turned her attention over to Mary. "Hello Mary," started the little old lady. Mary knew her from a few parties of her parent's during her youth. "Hello," Mary returned.

"I was sorry to hear about your loss," she said.

"Thank you."

The conversation ended with that, and the little old lady made her way back to her mother. Mary stopped her lips from shaking and reminded herself that she had made progress with that simple conversation, but the thought did not last as she remembered how many hundreds of more times she would have to hear someone bring up her loss. Mary felt her emotions taking control, but she breathed deep again, and reminded herself that experience could not hurt her, only her interpretations. She was able to calm herself just in time for the service to start. Mary felt tense but her father looked at her with reassuring eyes, and she was able to relax just a bit off the edges.

The rest of the service went by without many problems. She had to stand and be greeted by a few more people, and had to hear the hurtful words, no matter the empathetic envelopes that they came in. Mary stayed strong though, reminding herself that, "I am in control. I am strong."

The service ended and Mary dealt with just a few more small encounters and she was on her way home. The entire ordeal seemed so overwhelming, and though Mary was on the verge of tears three or four times with the mention of her passed children, she kept herself calm and held her head high. She was dressed in black, of course, but she didn't feel like mourning with tears in public, and, pleased with herself, she did not. The rest of Mary's day went by without any other ordeals and she spent the day thinking about what she would do with her life after she could handle people. And in between deep thoughts of where she would be useful, Mary would turn to her journal and write about her day and her thoughts at the moment. She spent time to put in detailed descriptions of the church and her feelings at the time, and if she remembered, details about the way her face looked at the time also.

Just as that Sunday passed without much trouble, Mary was able to go through the rest of the week with more control over her mind then even a week before. She even had her friend Pam over for another lunch, and she felt stronger and more empowered than before. Mary would still feel much sadness over the loss of her children, and though it pained her so, to look at the photos in her lock-it, she forced herself several times a day to think of them. Many times she would just pace back and forth holding the heart in her fist and praying to God to give her comfort and happiness. Mary still cried once a day, mostly with her thoughts of her children, but at every occurrence, Mary would remind herself that crying over her loss was not a bad thing to do, as the Doctor had told her.

Wednesday came again, and once more Mary looked forward to her session with the doctor. She walked into his office for the first time with a smile on *her* face. The doctor was nearly startled to see it as he smiled back to her.

"Hello Mary, and I would ask you how your day is, but I'm sure that it is going well."

"It is," she confessed.

"How was church," he asked, assuming directly after looking at her smile."

"Church was hard, but at least I went." She was almost startled at his clairvoyance, but she quickly realized that she was smiling. That wasn't the normal look for her.

"True. Tell me about the experience."

"It was tough, and I almost lost control a couple of times, but I kept in control."

"Splendid, Mary. Good job. How does it make you feel to have accomplished all of those short-term goals that I proposed three weeks ago?"

"It feels good," Mary responded with a slight smile. "I think that I'm on my way."

"I'm glad. Did you think about what you plan to do once you go back to work?"

"I did think about it. I thought about it for hours Doc, but I didn't come up with anything."

"You had a job waiting tables before. Do you think you would want to do that again?"

"No. It was hard when I didn't have the added worries that I have now. I'm not sure that I could handle such a stressful job."

"That is okay," he replied. "It is good that you have an idea of where your emotions lie and your ability to control them. I read this notebook of yours," he said taking out her last journal. "It is very precise, and I can't wait to read this other one, if you will let me, of course?"

"Yes," she said handing him the journal.

He looked over it briefly as he had the week prior, and similar to the last time his simple response was, "Wow." She looked up at him, glad that he had given it such high praise.

"Hey Doc, since you are taking that one, do you happen to have another empty one that I can continue on while you are reading that one?"

"Of course," he stated reaching into his desk to take hold of another notebook.

The rest of the session went by and the doctor stressed one point with much enthusiasm. He wanted her to remember that throughout her day and her life that small things cannot end her life or her happiness. And also, to make sure that when she feels overwhelmed with something that seems dangerous, to think about the true danger that it poses and look at every situation with logic. With those words of optimism the session ended and Mary went on her way home.

As she rode in the car with her father she peered out the window and looked at the sky, as she did often, to remind herself that she still had long in her life. Although she did not know where it would go from there, she knew that she would be happy again. She took comfort in it and she waited anxiously to get home and write in her journal about her thoughts and her day. And when the car drove up, she took no time to talk with her parents as there would be plenty of time for that in her life, and she went up stairs to write.

Her week passed by quickly, with another lunch with Pam, and hours of writing in her journal. Mary made an effort to talk with her parents more, and it was beginning to feel good, like it had when she was younger. She liked to be able to talk with her parents like she could talk with Doctor Ross. Her week was not one of fraught and sadness, but one with hope and tiny bits of joy finding its way into her heart every now and then. Of course, she still cried over her loss, but she felt stronger than she had in years even. Her heart felt like it was released from years of captivity. She wrote furiously in her journal and soon it was Wednesday again. The hour came and she went to her therapist once more.

The session went by with the same workings that always took place, him asking her questions about how she felt in the situations of her week, reminding her that crying over her children was healthy and proper, and that she was doing well in all aspects of her treatment. But as time would have it, the conversation drifted to her plans for the nearing future once more.

"Mary have you thought about your plans?"

"Yes, I've thought but still, I have yet to come up with a good idea."

"I read over your thoughts in this notebook," he said handing it to her. "You have a knack for writing. I have a friend over in the newspaper; he is actually editor in chief. He is looking for a column writer. I can have an appointment set up for you, if you would like?"

"I'm not sure," she began. "I have never been good at writing."

"This writing on your thoughts is very good," he rebutted. "And the sheer volume is impressive."

"Sure, but that is my mind on paper. Those are my thoughts and feelings."

"Tell him that, and he might just have something for you."

"I don't know if I could do it. Would I have to spend a lot of time there in the building, or could I do some work at home?"

"I'm sure that he could make something up for you. He is a good man."

"I don't know. What do you think, Doc?"

"Mary, I think that you would be a very good writer, but I can't make this decision for you. It would not be that much pressure. Although you would have time limits, I'm sure that for the first while he would be able to cut you some slack while you got the hang of it."

"Okay, I guess. I think that I could do this. I'm still not sure though," she stated.

"Well, how about meeting with him, and then go from there?"

"I can do that." Mary was still reluctant, but not because of the specifics of the job, but she wasn't sure if she was ready. But once more, the Doctor had his overwhelming and inspiring optimism.

"Okay, well, how is Monday morning for you at his office?" he asked.

"Whoa, okay, I can do that. Do I need to bring anything?"

"No, just yourself. I am not allowed to tell him anything about you, due to patient doctor privilege. I just simply said that I might know someone that might do well if he was looking for a writer. But I'm sure that you will do fine."

Mary soon left from the session, and was filled with mixed feelings. She was not sure of how well she would do, but the doctor's optimism seemed to be correct at many other problems, maybe he was right here too.

Mary went through her week in mixed feelings and anxiety. She was able to pound out another church service, and just as before, she was able to control her feelings and not allow her emotions to get the best of her. But before she knew it, Monday morning came.

At nine o'clock she waited outside of his office, trying not to make conversation with anyone. She felt so nervous. She second-guessed her dress, and she was frightened. The door opened and she was summoned inside and she breathed in a deep breath and made a quick prayer. "Please God, help me through this. Help me to be stronger than I had thought I could be."

"Hello Mary, how are you today?"

"I'm well, thank you."

"I'm glad to hear it. My name is Philip Sheridan. Doctor Ross told me that you might be good for the job I'm looking for. I'm sorry about your loss. We ran a small article about you when it happened, and if I blurt out something that I shouldn't about it, please hit me very hard," he said with a smile. Mary smiled for a brief second, but was still very nervous. "So Mary, tell me about yourself, more specifically any writing experience, or what type of writing you are good at."

"Well," she said with her lips trembling. "I don't have any writing experience and I am only good at writing about what I feel, or what I think. To be honest with you, I'm not sure about how well I could do at this job."

"Okay," he started again. "I'm glad to hear your honesty. I feel that I must tell you how much stock I put in the opinion of Doctor Ross. How do you think that you would do with something like a 'Dear Mary' type of thing, where people write to you about their problems and you give them an answer? It is a pretty simple thing, and most small newspapers have something like it just for kicks. If you do well and you would like to continue, then of course we can advance you to something more important, but if it is feelings that you like to write about then this may be your niche."

"I'm not sure if I could heal other people's problems. I can hardly take care of my own," she confessed.

"Well, how about I give you a couple questions from another paper or something, and you write down what you think they should do, and then give it back to me when you are done. Just do as much as you would like. I just need an idea of where you are. Do you think that you can have it done by tomorrow morning, this same time?"

"I think I can, yes sir."

"Terrific, Mary," he said handing her some old newspaper clippings. "I will see you tomorrow morning. Oh, do you need a computer or anything to type on?"

"My father has one."

"Okay then. I look forward to tomorrow."

Mary left with more worry in her heart than all of the last couple of weeks combined. She didn't know if she could write this by tomorrow, Hell she didn't even know if she could write it in a week. But as she got home, something inside her just clicked and she remembered her times as a student. She had forced herself through harder assignments, and she headed up to her room to look over the letters left by people. Unluckily, there were no responses, but only letters.

Mary spent all day looking through them, and by nightfall she had thought about each one, but still did not have any ideas what she would write, or even on which "Dear Abby." Mary's time was running out, but at eleven o'clock after her parents had gone to bed, she walked down to her father's office, and turned on

the computer. She opened a file and just let herself go.
She typed out the letter on the screen first:

Dear Abby,

 I'm having trouble with my fiancée. At
first we had so much in common, but now it
seems that we are slipping apart. I love him,
and I don't want to lose him, but I'm worried
about the future. Should I hold on and try to
work things out, or should I let go and try my
luck again elsewhere?

Sincerely,
Confused Sally.

 Mary looked at the words on the screen and
thought of her husband. She stopped thinking and just
began to write:

Dear Confused Sally,

 There is nothing else in life that people
try so hard to find than a soul mate. Whether
this man is right for you is not something that I
can answer, but something that you must
decide. Love is not just a graph of the good
and bad traits and then just go with the
majority, but a feeling that changes the way
that we look at life. If that man has found a
way to make you see life as a good thing, no
matter the troubles that have found their way
into your life, then the relationship is worth

many days of work. Look at yourself in his arms. If you feel like nothing can ever make him take those arms away from you, and you have no fear of him leaving you when the going gets tough, then your love may just be pure. I cannot tell you to stay with him, and I cannot tell you to leave, but if he looks you in the eyes and you feel nothing more than happiness, then hold on to what you have. There is something worse than loving a person and experiencing Heaven, but then going through Hell as they leave. The worse thing is never having a chance to find Heaven or Hell, and regret is the worst feeling of all that we can feel. Trust your heart, and you will find your Heaven.

Sincerely,
Mary

The next morning came and Mary shivered as he read over the article. The man read over it a couple of times and then he set it down on the desk and looked her in the eyes. Mary thought that he was going to act nice but tell her that she would not fit in at the place, and she shivered in anticipation of his voice.

"Mary, this is not the best writing I have ever seen. It does not appeal to me as a literary critic and it is not chopped full of huge words to make the readers pull out their dictionaries. I love it! Mary, this is your heart and soul put down on paper, and no person's heart or soul speaks to them in perfect iambic pentameter or overwhelming symbolism. Mary, I want to give you a job here."

Mary's heart nearly skipped a beat. She could hardly believe that words flowed from his mouth. She could say nothing.

"We don't have any letters here, of course, since it is not out yet. So you will have to make up your own "Letters to Mary," but I'm sure that you will do fine. I want to help you out anyway that you would like. You can have a laptop to work at any place and at any time, or you can work in the office, or you can do a combination of them all."

"Okay," she sounded. "I can do that."

The meeting ended shortly after as he explained to her of how many she needed to produce and by when. He had someone bring her a laptop with all of the accessories and she was given a desk space in the office also. Mary was overwhelmed by it all, and as she made thoughts that she was not sure if she could handle the pressure or not, she reminded herself of her strength and the day ended with her head on a pillow and a smile on her face.

The next day came and Mary found herself at Doctor Ross' office at the normal time. He was standing and asked her to come in. He did not take a seat as he smiled at her.

"I talked with my friend. How do you feel about working there?"

"I'm not sure, but I am somewhat excited. I am sure that I can do it. I know that I will have problems, and I know that it will be hard, but I think that I can handle this."

"That is great, Mary."

"Why are we standing?" she interrupted.

"Because you are done here," he said.

"What?" she asked startled.

"You have everything that you need. I would love for you to come by at any time that you think that you need a check-up, but you have every tool that you need to go on with the rest of your life. You are strong and courageous."

"Okay," she complied. She began to walk out the door through the lobby with her confused dad.

"What is wrong?" he asked.

"Nothing Daddy. I'm okay," Mary said with a smile.

They began to walk out of the front door and Doctor Ross quickly said something. "Mary, don't ever forget," as she turned her head to look at him. "You are strong, and you are in control of your happiness. Good luck." He smiled at him, and she smiled back.

As the two got into the car and headed home, Mary looked out her window and noticed the blue sky. Although the cold air found its way through the window, Mary was optimistic of the future. She didn't know if she would ever marry again, and she didn't know if she would ever have any children ever again. She didn't know if her job would work out, but it all seemed okay. She wanted to be happy. Mary pulled out her lock-it, held it tight and smiled.

Collin May

About the Author

Collin May lives in Ft. Worth, Texas. Collin has enjoyed writing since the day he learned how to write. He is a strong supporter of psychotherapy without the use of medication. He is currently studying psychology and plans to start his own practice based from a cognitive-behavioral perspective. His time spent away from school and work is filled with his close friends, running, or kayaking.